MEMORIES FROM MAPLE STREET

U.S.A:

PAWPRINTS ON MY HEART

Gayle M. Irwin
Ann Swann
Carol Huff
Sarah J. McNeal
Charlie Steel
C.J. Samuels
Jim Landwehr
Cher'ley Grogg
Beverly Wells
Carol Huff
Gil McDonald
Meg Mims
Tina Holt
Tanya Hanson
Cheryl Pierson
L.D.B. Taylor

Table of Contents

Lessons from Dogs—A Tribute

Gayle M. Irwin

"The road to my heart is paved in pawprints." This sign hangs on my living room wall. For me, no truer words were ever written or spoken. Since I was a child, animals have captured my heart, from dogs and cats to zebras and koalas. As a youngster and then a teenager, I collected posters of animals, in particular the exotics I'd never see in the wild, such as tigers and mountain lions. I was a huge cat fan for most of my younger years, a fan of both wild and domestic felines; my first pet was a cat I found as a stray when I was seven years old. However, after I received my first dog as a teenager, both canines and felines became my focus, and I've been loving and helping dogs and cats ever since.

After my husband and I said goodbye to the second dog we had together, a cocker spaniel named Cody, I reflected heavily upon the lessons people can learn from dogs. Cody was nearly 18 years old at the time of his passing. We adopted him in 2008 as a then nearly-10-year-old that had been used as a puppy mill stud and then discarded like yesterday's trash.

He was brought to our local humane society by a Good Samaritan who wanted to keep him but couldn't, due to her housing situation. When Cody came to live with us, my husband Greg and I figured we'd give him a great life for his last few years. Those two or three years turned into nearly eight, speaking to the perseverance and loyalty that dogs possess.

Those life lessons were also demonstrated by the Springer Spaniel we adopted from a Montana animal shelter in 2001. A papered purebred named Sage, she became totally blind by the age of three due to Progressive Retinal Atrophy (PRA), a genetic disease for which there is no cure. She adapted well to losing her sight, something not every dog—nor every human—does; she even survived being lost in a mountainous forest for three days. Courage, perseverance, self-confidence, flexibility—these, and many other lessons, are what I learned from Sage. I share those and other lessons as a writer and a speaker.

I am honored to be a part-time freelance writer. I compose magazine articles, newspaper columns, and blog posts. I'm a contributor to six *Chicken Soup for the Soul* anthologies and have authored seven books. Most of my stories reflect some aspect of pet ownership and the lessons humans can learn from animals. I also speak in schools, at libraries, and for civic and faith-based organizations. My goal in these endeavors is to encourage and inspire people—animals help me accomplish that.

Over the years, I've learned much from pets. So, here is a little tribute to Cody and Sage and to all pets who touch our lives about the lessons people can learn from them.

Courage—Sage exhibited a courage that was inspirational. Unable to see, she jumped on the couch, up on the bed, and also onto chairs. I referred to those acts as "leaps of faith." I don't know if I'd be brave enough to jump upon something or to navigate a set of stairs that I couldn't see. But, she did that daily. Sage also showcased courage when she was lost for three days in the woods. Blind and alone, she survived in an area where black bears and mountain lions reside. Although I'll never know exactly how—except for the grace of a loving Creator—she lived through the experience, and Greg and I were able to find her and bring her home safe. From that spawned *Sage's Big Adventure—Living with Blindness,* a chapter book that has captured the hearts of both children and adults. The story reminds us all that animals are brave and they have value, no matter their abilities or disabilities—and that lesson applies to people, as well.

Tenacity—Again, Sage's life is such a testimony; so is Cody's. He lived to an age many dogs don't. He had major health issues, starting when he was about 13 years old, including nearly dying from an autoimmune disease. But, he rebounded, and he pushed through the many setbacks thereafter, including tearing his ACL. His heart remained strong to the very end, one of the reasons making that "tough decision" was even more difficult. However, his other issues, including kidney and liver failure, and painful cornea problems, were too much for his aging body to tackle, and ultimately the reasons our veterinarian said, "It's time."

Friendship—Dogs and other pets give us the best in friendship: devotion and love with no strings attached—unless you count food and shelter! I've never known a human to wait at the door or window for me to come home—not even my husband or parents do that! A wagging tail, an excited bark, a grab of a favorite toy brought to and placed at one's feet...each and every warm greeting is the supreme act of faithfulness and friendship. Dogs stay with us through sickness as well as health, something many *people* don't do, even when they vow they will during a marriage ceremony. When we suffer from illness, many times our pets will lie next to us, or nearby. Dogs are also in tune to our emotional health and will often lie beside us or place their head on our knee when we're discouraged, or anxious. Because of their sensitivity and affection, therapy dogs are welcomed into hospitals, nursing homes, and schools. Dogs give us the best gift in life: themselves.

Sacrifice—Sometimes, that ultimate gift is the dog's demise. Canines save people from fire, avalanches, and criminals. They go to war with American servicemen and women, and often, like these brave people, the dogs' lives are sacrificed for our freedom. K-9 handlers have lost their four-footed partners in the line of duty, and families lose their beloved pet—but still have their children—because the dog came between the child and a snake, bear, or other predatory animal. A blind woman was saved by her guide dog when a bus barreled down on the pair, and the dog stepped between the motoring unit and his beloved human. "No greater love has anyone than this: to lay down his life for another..." Dogs do that.

Contentment—The lifestyle of many western cultures demands we *do* more, and *get* more. Moving up the ladder of career, possessing the latest technological gadget, and buying the best automobile has kept people enslaved to big businesses, especially retail stores, credit card companies, and banks. Simplicity is frowned upon, even though it means more financial freedom. And yet, with all the "stuff", we can still be discontented. A dog's life is simple: shelter, food, water, exercise, and companionship satisfies our canine friends. Humans can learn a lot from their dog's simple joys—chasing a butterfly, running through a field, sharing time with friends, or basking in the warmth of sunlight—and in being content with the smaller, simpler things in life.

Rest—Dogs know when to play and when to rest. Sleep is needed for health, yet many people don't get the rest they need to recover from illness or from a hard day at work. We are on the go constantly, driving ourselves and our children hither and yon, filling our "life plate" so full we can't keep up with ourselves. From those exploits and over-extensions, our emotional and physical health suffers. Dogs sleep at night, they wind down after exercise, and they nap during the day. Spending time resting and in quiet helps relax us physically, and detoxifies us mentally. If only we'd do so more often, like our dogs.

There are numerous other great life lessons people can learn from dogs. One of those is sharing: the sharing of affection, of time, of caring and compassion, of experiences. There is also the lesson of loss. Dogs live an average of 10 years; bigger breeds, like Great Danes, don't usually make it to that age, while smaller breeds, such as toy poodles, can live to be 20 or more. Loss comes to each of us, to our family, to our friends, to our pets.

Like our dogs, who also seem to grieve over a friend's passing—whether that companion be another furry one or a human one—we mourn and we move on. Love can come again if our hearts are open. When you think of the numerous dogs in rescues and shelters needing new homes, those who have lost human companions to nursing homes, or to death, remember how they open their hearts to new human owners, to new pet friends, to life itself. Cody and Sage exemplified that, adapting, trusting, and loving despite loss and grief. Most dogs do.

I am thankful for the gift of my pets, each and every one, from childhood to middle age. I am also thankful for the gift of writing, the passion for writing, and the desire to share the lessons and joys of having pets. Although Sage and Cody are both gone from this earth, their legacy will live on in my books and stories. In that fact, and in the memories I have of my beloved dogs, I find joy and gratitude. My heart certainly has pawprints etched all through it!

About the Author—Gayle M. Irwin

Gayle M. Irwin is an award-winning Wyoming writer. She is the author of several inspirational dog stories for children and adults, and she freelances for newspapers and magazines.

Gayle has contributed stories to six different *Chicken Soup for the Soul* books, including the 2014 release *The Dog Did What?*, and the recently released *The Spirit of America*, in which she has written about America's national parks. She supports various pet rescue organizations, and regularly speaks in schools, at libraries, and for civic and faith-based groups.

Learn more about Gayle and her writing and speaking endeavors at www.gaylemirwin.com.

Snakeman

Ann Swann

When we lost Droopy to distemper, Mom vowed not to get another puppy. We were not rich, and she'd spent a whole week's grocery money at the vet trying to save him. Besides, the sight of our poor little shepherd under her bed, convulsing with fever, would stay with us forever.

But then came Snake.

He was a good-sized pup. Half boxer, half pit bull, he came to our family from a young man whose new apartment complex didn't allow pets. Apparently, it was either us or the pound.

The stout brown pup stole our hearts from day one. Just like a kid, he got in as much trouble as any of us—maybe even more. Then, he got sick. We didn't know the distemper virus lived on in the dirt of our yard. Even after six weeks.

And we didn't have any more money for the vet. But Mom was determined. She did for him what she did for any of us when we got a respiratory infection. She rubbed his chest with menthol rub, wrapped him in a blanket, and fed him chicken soup—and lots of it.

His real name was Simon—at least, that's what the previous owner said—but my stepdad, Bull, gave him the nickname Snake-hips because after he recovered, that dog was so happy to be alive he wiggled all over. But Snake-hips didn't really stick. It quickly morphed into Snake, Snaker, Snakeman, or even The Snake.

The vet said Mom's cure didn't really save him. He said most likely the virus was weak and the dog simply much stronger and slightly older than poor little Droopy had been. *Whatever.* We knew Mom saved him. Snake knew it, too. Over the years, he proved time and again that he was our special protector. We all fell under his jurisdiction. Maybe it was just a trait of his breed(s), but we didn't think so.

He was different. Special. Before long, he even became a favorite of Mrs. McGuire, the wealthy widow lady who lived across the street. That surprised us all, given the fact that Snake's favorite pastime was chasing her feral cats through the park-like setting of her huge yard.

Mom tried to apologize for him each time she dragged him home, but Mrs. McGuire wasn't the least bit put off.

She said it was all okay, because he never actually caught the cats. He only wanted to play. She seemed convinced the animal shenanigans were nothing more than fun and games.

In fact, over the years, she became so smitten with that dog she sent him a personal invitation to her granddaughter's fifth birthday party. After some debate, Mom allowed him to go. She was rewarded with photos of him sitting at Mrs. McGuire's immense dining table with his party hat on and his cake and ice cream on a china plate before him. Mom said, "I hope she at least put plastic under his butt. Those chairs look like they're covered in *damask*."

There were several smiling little girls seated around the table, all dressed in their birthday finery, and then there were a couple of other pictures that showed him chasing bubbles and popping balloons. In every photo that silly dog was still wearing his crooked party-cone hat. And every single photo was labeled Solomon. We don't know if she simply misunderstood his real name all those years, or whether he told her that *was* his real name. They had quite the connection, that much I do know.

One day, a new dogcatcher arrived in our area. Right away, he spied the Snake keeping watch over our North Sixth Street neighborhood. Mom said it was the funniest thing she'd ever seen when she looked out the front door and saw Snaker headed for home with the dogcatcher hot on his tail. That's not what tickled her funny bone, though; it was Mrs. McGuire, that sweet southern lady, who dashed out in the street, flagged the new man down, and read him the riot act right there in front of God and everybody. Mom said that dainty little old woman's white hair was flying almost as wildly as the curse words. Needless to say, Snake was spared a trip to the pound.

Perhaps as a way of showing his gratitude, The Snake brought home one of Mrs. McGuire's wild cats and kept it for a pet. The old tom had a dull yellow-striped coat and a crooked tail. He sauntered right into our living room between Snake's front legs. The dog wouldn't come in without the cat. They were quite a sight sitting together on Mom and Bull's bookcase headboard watching out the window for "Naddy"—our nickname for Daddy—to come home from work.

The Beatles arriving at New York's Kennedy Airport in 1964 had nothing on Bull when he came through that side door. We'd yell "Naddy, Naddy, Naddy," and the fur would fly. Snake always led the charge with Julie the dachshund, Mr. Dee, the poodle, and now Tom, the cat, making up the entourage. Plus us kids, of course. But who could hear us over all the yips, howls, and meows?

Bull wasn't the only rock star in the family, though. To Snake, Mom shared top billing, too. They went almost everywhere together in our nondescript white Plymouth with the clear, bubbly-textured plastic seat covers.

At the Piggly Wiggly, Mom would park, roll down all the windows and go inside. If Snake got tired of waiting in the car, he would jump out and sit by the big glass double doors. When he saw her coming, he would hop back in the car.

One day, Mom came out just as Snake jumped back in the passenger window. She stowed her groceries in the back seat, got in and stuck her key in the ignition. But the key would not turn. That's when she noticed a pair of blue baby booties hanging from the rearview mirror. Mom didn't have any little boys. She knew right away what had happened. The Snake had jumped into the wrong car. Mom said she cussed him the whole time she was unloading and reloading her groceries into her identical car two spaces away. She admitted she prayed the owners of the booties would not come out and catch her taking her own groceries out of their car.

She got lucky that time. No one caught her. But she said that wasn't nearly as embarrassing as the day a woman across town called her on the phone and asked her if she owned a large brown dog named Snake.

When Mom confessed she was the owner, the lady asked her to please come and remove said dog from her kitchen. It seemed he'd fallen in love with her English bulldog and simply followed her right in through the doggy door from their backyard. Not only did we have difficulty keeping him inside our own cinder block fence, it was also difficult to keep him *out* of anyone else's fence.

"He's very well-mannered," the lady told Mom on the phone. "But I can't convince him it's time to leave. He just sits there looking at me with those big brown eyes." Mom said the lady chuckled self-consciously when she said, "I'm glad you put the phone number on his tag. I knew his name, but not his number."

Mom didn't even ask the woman *how* she knew his nickname. On his tag, it said Simon. When she hurried to the woman's house to retrieve him, she said Snake strolled right out the front door and leapt in the passenger window of the old Plymouth as if he'd simply been waiting for his chauffeur to arrive.

I don't know why we never installed a doggy door. Maybe the folks were afraid Snake would bring girls home, or adopt more strays like old Tom. Nothing in the neighborhood escaped his attention. He even patrolled our rooftop once he discovered he could climb the brick waterfall in the backyard, walk the length of the fence, and make the short leap from the well house to the steep slant of the attached garage. Seeing him perched on the edge of the shingles like a furry gargoyle was always quite a sight.

Although Mom was embarrassed by his actions from time to time, she usually got away unscathed. Bull's brother, Uncle Joe, was not so fortunate. Snake got revenge on him in the most appropriate way.

In the warmer months, Uncle Joe always wore a white straw cowboy hat. Being ornery, he would sometimes use that hat to whack Snakeman in the face and tease him.

"You'll regret that someday," Bull told him.

Sure enough, someday finally came.

It was high summer when Uncle Joe stopped by for a visit one afternoon. He was standing in the yard with Bull, chewing the fat, white hat held loosely against his leg, when, out of nowhere, Snakeman barreled past. Without a pause, old Snake snatched the hat out of Uncle Joe's hand, ran off a short distance and tore that evil thing to shreds. Then he looked up, chest heaving, pieces of the brim dangling from his jaws, and stared right at Uncle Joe as if to say, "Whaddya think about *that*?"

Shaking his head, Uncle Joe simply got in his car and drove away.

Bull walked back to the house, grinning. I'm not absolutely certain, but I think I heard him mutter, "I told you."

It was about this time that the idea of reincarnation crossed my mind. I wondered if Snake might've been a

13

teenage boy in another life. He had quite a thing for cars. His favorite napping spot was on top of the old Plymouth.

Once, he even got to drive.

Blonde and blue-eyed, my sister, Jay, had lots of teenaged suitors. Old Snakeman loved to help her greet them all. If the weather were cold or rainy, he would sometimes go to the door wearing his windbreaker with the hood up like the doggy Unabomber. If one of the guys tried to skip the official greeting and just drive up to the curb for a sit 'n' visit, well, The Snake was liable to take part in that, too.

One evening, Jay's friend, Dean, and his brother came over. It was still summertime, so Snake wasn't wearing his hoodie, but since the boys' old Chevy didn't have air conditioning, all the windows were rolled down. Dean was acquainted with Snake, but his younger brother, Tony, had only heard rumors. For some reason, they called our dog Godzilla. I think Tony assumed he would be safe staying in the car while Dean came up to the door.

Snake must've already been outside when he heard the car idling at the curb. Who knows? He may have been watching from the roof. Without warning, he sidled up to the vehicle and hopped in the passenger window. Tony didn't even stop to put the hand brake on. He just slid out the driver's side door and let the dog have it.

I don't know if Tony knocked the car in gear when he slid out, or whether Snakeman actually found first on purpose, but however it happened, for a few minutes that dog was driving down the street. Naturally, he drove past Mrs. McGuire's house. The show-off. He was probably headed to his English girlfriend's place, but I guess we'll never know. Tony ran to the door yelling, "Help!

Godzilla's stealing my car!"

Fortunately, the dog couldn't reach the accelerator. Jay and Dean caught him before he made it to the corner.

Another time he almost got us in trouble was the afternoon Jay and I were goofing around in Mom and Bull's bedroom while they were gone. We were like Thing 1 and Thing 2, giving each other piggyback rides, falling backward onto their huge king-sized bed, and generally cutting up and acting stupid.

Of course, Snaker heard the commotion and decided he wanted to play, so the next time I leapt on Jay's back, Snake leapt up against her chest and knocked the pair of us backward into the wall. The combined weight of two teenage girls and one large dog made a person-sized hole in the sheetrock.

I'll never forget how quickly we scrambled away from that hole with our hands covering our mouths. Brilliant thinkers, we pushed a thin metal bookshelf in front of the damage and hoped for the best.

The next day, Bull said, "Girls, what the hell happened to my bedroom wall?"

Naturally, we blamed the whole thing on poor old Snakeman. And just like Uncle Joe, Bull simply shook his head and cut his losses. It was hard to argue with the four-legged kid—he never talked back.

Next time, I'll tell you about the day Mom baked brownies for my classroom and set them to cool in the middle of her new dinette. The table still bears the dog-claw scars—and one of the chairs didn't survive at all. But that was a long time ago.

I sure miss those days. I miss that old dog. He had a good long life thanks to Mom and menthol rub, and we all learned a new level of grief when his big heart gave out at the age of twelve. The vet said that was old age for a dog his size, but we didn't agree. No matter the years, it never would have been enough.

Now, I'm just thankful that young man's apartment complex didn't allow pets. I can't imagine what would have filled up the giant hole in our lives if old Snaker hadn't come along.

About the Author—Ann Swann

Ann Swann was born in the small West Texas town of Lamesa. She grew up much like the title character in her *Stevie-girl and the Phantoms* series (though she never got up the nerve to enter the haunted house). Ann has done everything from answering 911 Emergency calls to teaching elementary school. She still lives in Texas with her husband and rescue pets. When she's not writing, Ann is reading. Her to-be-read list has grown so large it has taken on a life of its own. She calls it Herman. The story of Snakeman is true. It is just one of many.

Sunny Delight

Carol Huff

I heard the sound of a shotgun echoing through the valley between my house and my neighbor's. I looked up at the clock and noticed the time—2:10 in the afternoon. *Wonder what's going on?*

Rising from my desk, I looked out the window facing the valley. It was then that I saw her for the first time, running for her life. With her tail tucked between her legs, the small yellow dog ran as fast as her short legs could carry her, stopping only after she made her way to the top of the hill in front of my office building, a good 300 feet in front of me.

I watched her as she settled down into a small heap, panting, with her head resting on her front paws as her eyes scanned the horizon.

Oh, no, another stray.

But it was really no surprise. The road behind my office is a graveled county road with no houses for miles, and it's the perfect spot for dropping off unwanted animals in a county where no animal shelter exists. Either my neighbor or I have always been the recipients of these strays who forage for food, water and kindness in an unkind world.

My neighbor, however, isn't as understanding as I am. He's taken in his share of strays, nursed them back to health if the expense wasn't too great, and then found loving homes for them—but only if it didn't require much effort on his part. *So, why had he fired the shot to scare this one off?*

I opened the door and made eye contact with the frightened creature lying on the hillside. From where I stood, I couldn't see the severity of her problems. I gently called to her and I watched as her tail started wagging. I coaxed her to head in my direction, anxious to see how friendly she was. She picked herself up from her prone position and stood looking at me, tail still wagging, probably wondering if it was safe to approach.

I went out onto the porch and opened the plastic bin where I kept dog food for just such emergencies. I poured out a generous helping of tasty morsels and proceeded toward her, encouraging her to trust me. We met halfway. It was only then that I understood my neighbor's reluctance to let her stay.

Her face was swollen from infection, her eyes nearly closed. Her neck was puffy and raw, and the fur was almost completely gone from her legs, face, and neck. *Mange!*

I'd never had any dealings with mange, and I was reluctant to touch her. I had my other dogs to think about. She, however, didn't know she had mange and her tongue drooled at the smell of the food I placed before her in the plastic bowl. She consumed it in five bites and then licked the bowl, her small face looking up at me for more.

I knew at that moment I would not let her suffer any longer. I went back inside and made a frantic call to my vet.

"I have a stray dog here, and she's covered with mange, I think. Can you see us this afternoon?"

"Any signs of rabies?"

"No, she appears normal in every other way."

"Will she let you touch her?"

"I haven't tried."

"Can you get her in your van?"

"I don't know anything at all about her, but I'll try."

"Bring her in if you can, or I can come to you. It's not the end of the world for her. Mange can be treated."

"What about my other dogs? Is she contagious to them?"

"It depends on what kind of mange it is. Let me have a look at her before you let the other dogs around her."

"I'll be there shortly."

That's all I needed to hear. I went back outside and gave her water, which she lapped appreciatively.

Poor baby. Someone's been so cruel to you. How will I get you in the van? I don't want to touch you because

19

you're covered with mange, and infection is dripping everywhere.

I started walking across the field to my house to get a clean towel to wrap around her. She followed me, close on my heels, probably hoping I wouldn't leave her behind like some other uncaring person had done. It was obvious to me that she had once known the touch of a human, but that human had deserted her in her time of need. They dropped her off on the deserted stretch of road and never looked back at her fearful eyes as she wondered where she was and why she was being left behind.

How could anyone do that? It's totally beyond my scope of comprehension. A person like that is born with a big hole in their chest where their heart is supposed to be.

Towel in hand, she and I walked back across the field to the utility van I used in my business. I opened the back door, placed the towel around her, and picked her up. She offered no resistance as I placed her in the back, and closed the door.

She probably thinks I'm going to drop her off on the side of the road like somebody else did.

The vet met me outside. He patted her on the head, looked at me and said, "Wow!"

"What's your opinion?" I asked.

"Red mange, most likely. I'll know shortly."

He took some skin scrapings from her neck and told me he'd be back in a few minutes.

While he was gone, she stared at me with hopeful eyes and wagged her bedraggled tail with no fur on it.

"You're going to be okay, girl. We're just trying to help you," I reassured her in a calm voice.

In just a few minutes, my vet returned and gave me a

sympathetic look as he said, "Yep, red mange."

"Can it be treated?" I asked.

"Yes, it can, but red mange is the hardest form to cure. We can get rid of the infection quickly by treating her with a high dose of antibiotics, but it'll take about a year for her hair to come back. She will have to have medicine daily for a while, then weekly for the rest of her life."

"Is she contagious?"

"She's not contagious to your other dogs because red mange is hereditary. It's in her blood. We can keep it under control, but she should never be allowed to have pups. We'll need to spay her as soon as we get the infection cleared up some."

"Is the treatment something I can do at home instead of transporting her day after day up here for you to do?" I asked.

Not that it would make any difference as to what his answer would be, because I knew I was not about to let this sweet girl suffer from something that was curable.

"Oh, no, you won't have to bring her to me. It's medicine that you give her orally once a day. Very simple process."

"OK, let's get started."

"Do you have a name picked out for her?"

A name?

I had no idea, because I wasn't expecting such a bundle of neediness to come knocking on my door. As I looked at her, her tail wagged in tune to my thoughts and I could see her smiling with her puffy eyes.

She's such a delightful girl. She's the color of a ray of sunshine.

"Sunny Delight."

"OK, let's get Sunny Delight inside to begin her

21

treatment," he replied as he picked her up and carried her gingerly through the door to his examination room. Her thin, bony body trembled as I reached and touched her head for the first time.

God, why does this happen to Your beautiful creatures? How can people be so mean?

The first week didn't go well for Sunny Delight. The medicine made her sick to her stomach, and every time I gave it to her, she threw it back up. I phoned my vet for advice.

"It's the most effective medicine on the market. Try giving her half of it in the morning and the other half in the late afternoon," he suggested.

I tried it, and she kept it down. So we kept up that pace. The next few months brought about great changes in Sunny D's appearance. With daily treatments of antibiotics, the infection went away. Her eyes began to look normal and bright as the puffiness subsided, and her fur started to grow over the once-raw skin. Every day brought about new changes, and our hope rose. She began to realize there was more to life than scratching herself all day long from the horrific itch caused by red mange. She developed a healthy appetite, but she no longer woofed down her food as if it would be her last meal. The scar from her spaying healed over nicely. Happiness emanated from her as she made friends with the other animals that called my rescue farm their home.

Six months into her treatment, Sunny D appeared to be sluggish and feverish. I rushed her to the vet, who diagnosed an upper respiratory infection. Different antibiotics were given to treat that particular problem, but we had to suspend her mange treatment for a few days in order for her to recover from the respiratory problem.

It seemed that we took one step forward and two steps backward. It wasn't long, however, until we were back on track with her mange treatment.

A year later, Sunny D shows almost no signs of red mange. She's a fat, healthy bundle of joy who lives up to her name daily. She greets me enthusiastically whenever she sees me and rides beside me in the golf cart as we check fences every day. Nothing goes unnoticed by her now-clear eyes. She chases butterflies through the meadows and barks at blue jays when they fly down at her. Her love for the farm pond goes without saying as she stands knee-deep in the water barking at the fish as they curiously nibble at her.

My neighbor, the one who shot up in the air to scare her away, saw her for the first time the other day as we rode through the pasture on the golf cart.

"Where'd you get the cute dog?" he asked, unaware of his shortcomings. "My kids would love her."

"Oh, she was a stray who adopted me," I told him.

Sometimes life just works out that way.

My heart swelled with pride as I looked over at her, sitting face forward, ready to take on any other demons that might possibly come her way. She's definitely my hero.

About the Author—Carol Huff

Carol Huff lives a hectic life as owner (and Chief Poop-Scooper) of Sudie Belle Animal Sanctuary in Hartwell, Georgia. She finds inspiration for her writing amongst the forty-plus rescued animals who call her farm home. She is a regular contributor to *Chicken Soup for the Soul*, and her stories have also been published in *Country Magazine, Guideposts, Readers Digest, Country Extra Magazine, The Brayer, Ploughshares*, and *Simply Southern Magazine*. Aside from writing, her hobbies include horseback riding, interior decorating, and sleeping.

The Wayfaring Stranger

Sarah J. McNeal

Growing up, we had many pets, some of them odd. Besides the usual dogs and cats, we had rabbits, birds, tadpoles, two spiny lizards, a baby alligator and, once, a snake. The snake lived in a terrarium-type enclosure Pop made for it that included a warming light. But it escaped its enclosure one day and we never found it again. After many sleepless nights of worrying it might slither into one of our beds, Mom declared there would be no more snakes as pets. We had a menagerie of pets with plenty of interesting stories around them, but nothing could have prepared us for the wayfaring stranger that would appear at our house years later.

****

On a perfectly ordinary autumn afternoon, Mom picked me up at school and told me about an amazing event that had happened to her that day.

"I heard a knock on the door, but when I went to see who it was, no one was there." She gave me a sideways glance that said *just wait, there's more to come.* "A few minutes later, I heard the knock again. At first, I didn't see anyone, but when I opened the door to get a better look, the screen door opened. I looked down to see who had opened it...and there was a monkey. Honest. It was a monkey. He opened the door, pretty as you please, and walked right in. I have no idea how that monkey knew how to open that door unless it had watched me open it to let the cat in."

She was starting to creep me out. Maybe she was getting ready to tell me the punchline to a joke. I relaxed, confident that the tall tale would soon come to an end and the grand finale would be revealed. I soon learned this was not to be, as Mom continued her foray into *The Twilight Zone.*

"I worried that Tiger [the cat] or Ember [the ridiculously silly dog] might attack him, so I lured him into the bathroom with pieces of bread." She laughed. "The poor thing was so hungry. And I noticed the ends of some of his fingers were missing. I suppose he must have been out in the cold for some time, and had gotten frostbite. He was so pitiful." She shook her head slightly as we pulled into the driveway.

I figured whatever was happening with my mother, she believed this story. She sure included a whole lot of details I wouldn't have expected in such a fantasy. The thought crossed my mind she might have overdosed on her heart meds. As soon as I got into the house, I knew I had to call Pop at work and tell him what was going on with Mom. He would know what to do.

First thing Mom did when we entered the house was to direct me to the bathroom where she'd put the alleged monkey. Cracking the door just enough to see inside, I gasped when I saw the furry thing licking a bar of soap. It was not the little monkey my mother had described. Instead, he was about two-and-a-half feet tall! And he was none too happy when I entered his domain.

He came up to me without the slightest fear, placed his hand on my knee, and bared his huge teeth at me— apparently, very unhappy with my presence.

Besides the fact that we had a monkey in our bathroom, what surprised me most was how disturbingly human he looked. I could read his facial expressions about as well as any human being's. His eyes expressed human-like emotion. In them, I could see his circumstances had brought about great pain and suffering for him. He was afraid...and lonely. I couldn't imagine what it must be like for him enduring such hardships without a companion to comfort him. He seemed to get upset when I gazed at him for very long, especially if I made eye contact, so I tried to just make covert glances.

How could scientists use these creatures for experiments? It would be like intentionally torturing a child.

Even though I realized Mom's story was completely true, confirming the old saying that truth is stranger than fiction, I still called Pop at work because I had no idea what we should do with the critter. My dad was a meteorologist and worked for the U.S. Weather Bureau stationed at the airport. He gave weather reports on the radio several times a shift, and had friends at several radio stations. Pop was certain the monkey was someone's pet that had escaped, and decided to contact his radio friends to tell people about the monkey in the hopes that the owner would come forward.

Now, I suppose I ought to mention here that my dad was a bit of a jokester. He liked to tell jokes and kid around with people. Naturally, his radio buddies thought he was messing with them so, when they announced the monkey missing in action, they also added their own take on the situation mentioning other sightings and things like Martians and UFOs flying into our backyard.

Neighbors began to line up at our door wanting to see the monkey—questioning in their minds, I'm certain, whether it really existed. It was kind of weird to have people coming through our house to see the monkey in the bathroom as if they were at the public zoo. I just want to inject here that nothing turns off the need to use the bathroom like a crowd of neighbors and strangers lined up at the bathroom door and a disgruntled monkey with big teeth occupying the inner sanctum of a place in which one would generally like to have some dang privacy. Just sayin'.

My friend, Jimmy, lived just down the street from our house. Of course, I wanted to tell him about the monkey occupying our bathroom right away. It was one of the most exciting things that ever happened to my family. Just like my response to my mother's story when she first told me about it, he did not believe me. He wanted to see the monkey for himself and said he would be over after supper to see it.

In the meantime, Pop came home from work and gave the monkey the once-over to see if it was healthy. He made the monkey a nice place to rest by cutting a door in a large cardboard box and put a blanket in it for him to warm up. Pop made sure the non-edible items such as razor blades, soap and toothpaste were removed and put a bowl of water and some food in the room for the monkey. I'm not positive, but I think the food consisted of a peanut butter and honey sandwich and an apple. He referred to the monkey as "Clem" after a TV character played by Red Skelton named Clem Kadiddlehopper. He noticed the missing fingertips, and affirmed Mom's assessment that it must be from frostbite. I felt sorry for the monkey. It must have suffered outside for a long time.

No one came forward to claim poor Clem. Obviously, we could not keep him in a bathroom and none of us knew how to properly care for a monkey. What were we going to do?

This was one of those times when it helped to have connections. My sister had a friend whose father had exotic birds. Mr. Metz kept his birds in a big compound that was heated in the cold months with huge cages that extended floor to ceiling for his birds. Better yet, the Metz family had once owned a pet monkey, and knew how to care for one.

Pop called Mr. Metz and told him about the monkey. He asked him if he would like to take Clem, and Mr. Metz readily agreed to give Clem a home. Soon, his daughter, Miriam, and her fiancé arrived and took Clem in a cardboard box to his new home. The crowd at our house finally dispersed, and the bathroom became a private sanctuary once again.

Not fifteen minutes after Clem left, Jimmy pulled into the driveway wanting to see the monkey that came to our house. Pop took one picture of Clem in his cardboard house, but the film was still in the camera and the slide would not appear for a couple of weeks. I had no proof of Clem's existence. It was a Big Foot situation.

A month or so later, I was able to show Jimmy the slide of Clem. Only then did he truly believe me.

I still find it incredible how all this drama happened in one afternoon. Sometimes, it's almost like a dream I had—except I still have that slide of Clem in his cardboard box. I seldom look at those slides now, but when I do and come across his picture, it always surprises me to remember what a wonderful experience that day brought.

Sometime after Clem had settled into his new home, Pop and I went to see how he was doing. Mr. Metz took us into the building where he kept his exotic flock of peacocks, Macaw parrots, and other feathered pets. There was Clem in his huge cage, playing on a swing. As soon as he saw Mr. Metz, he got very excited. I could tell he was happy to see him. Mr. Metz gave him a peppermint stick, which Clem immediately began to lick with uninhibited enthusiasm. I'm certain it tasted better than the soap he licked at our house.

"He loves peppermint," Mr. Metz explained. He smiled when he watched Clem swing around his quarters with the candy cane in his mouth. While Mr. Metz and Pop talked, Clem went to the side of his cage and shook the bars. When the birds started to squawk and squeal, it sounded like Clem was laughing. Mr. Metz chuckled. "He loves to stir up the birds for fun." Pop and I laughed, watching Clem's antics.

On the way back to the car, Pop and I talked about how happy Clem seemed and what a piece of luck it was that the monkey chose our house to visit that day. It felt good to know that we had something to do with Clem finding the happiness he so deserved.

****

Years later, when I worked in coronary care, I had a patient who told me about a train that derailed in Pageland, South Carolina, forty-two miles from Charlotte, North Carolina, where we lived. He said a circus car of monkeys was damaged in the accident and some of the monkeys escaped from it into the neighborhood. The residents never knew if they found all the monkeys, but he felt certain the ones they didn't find probably died in the cold winter that followed. I realized that the timing was about right for Clem's escape. I told him about Clem, and we both agreed that Clem was probably one of those monkeys that broke out of the train car.

All I could think was what a tough and brave little guy Clem was to make his way all those miles without being hit by a car or killed by a dog or a frightened person. How ingenious of him to have somehow managed to find food and water to sustain himself until he came to our house. It really made me happy to know he had found a forever home, and that my family played a little part in his rescue from a life that could have had a grim outcome. The mystery of Clem seemed solved and his story had come full circle. I will always remember with affection and admiration our little wayfaring stranger who managed to survive against all odds through courage and tenacity until he found a home and love.

About the Author—Sarah J. McNeal

Sarah J. McNeal is a multi-published author of time travel, paranormal, western, contemporary and historical fiction. Her stories may be found at Prairie Rose Publications and its imprints: Fire Star Press, Painted Pony Books, and Sundown Press and Publishing by Rebecca Vickery. You may find her at **Facebook** Her website: **http://www.sarahmcneal.com**

My Cat Stella

Charlie Steel

It was the summer of 1953. I was eight years old when a half-grown gray-striped cat showed up at the back door. It was late Sunday afternoon and the poor kitty was meowing pitifully when Dad and I opened the door. Taking an old bowl, my father poured milk into it and set it on the back porch. The furry little thing attacked the milk with her tongue and lapped away until the bowl was empty. My mother came to see what was going on, and as usual, put her foot down.

"I won't have a dirty old cat in the house!"

"I can fix a box for it under the porch, Mom," I said.

"She's a cute little thing," said my father, a huge grin on his face. "Suppose we call her Stella."

"Oh, Glenn!" declared my mother in an exasperated voice as she walked away.

It wasn't until years and years later when I saw *A Streetcar Named Desire* and heard Marlon Brando scream out, *"Hey, Stella!"* that I understood the inside joke and my father's sense of humor.

"It's not a boy?" I asked.

"No, son," said my dad picking the kitten up and turning it over to make sure. "When cats come in this color, they're usually females."

I spent the rest of the afternoon playing with Stella out on the grass. Called for dinner and not wanting to lose my new-found friend, I put her in a box and carried her down to the basement. I knew it was a serious offense, but I dared to break Mother's rules. I closed the basement stairs door, as well as the one into the kitchen, so no one would hear the poor little thing mewing away down there. Like many parents of that era, my mother believed pets were a luxury—and, in any case, belonged outside—not in the house.

After supper, I snuck several small pieces of chicken down to my new cat. To my delight, she devoured the meat. Then, just before dark, I found a bunch of rags and an old baby blanket. These, I put in the box to make a soft bed for my new pet.

Later, when I knew Mother would not hear, I returned to the basement, got Stella and the box, and climbed the stairs to the back porch. Under the old wooden porch steps was a square hole leading into the crawl space. I managed to stuff the box inside and then placed the kitten on the soft cloths. Stella began meowing fiercely, and as the sun set, I left her alone and went back into the house.

As much as I wanted the cat in my bedroom, I didn't dare bring the kitty in the house and further defy Mother's orders. The best I could do was hope my new pet would be there in the morning. To help make it so, I had one more idea. I found the old bowl, went to the refrigerator and poured milk into it. Unfortunately, Mother was there.

"Young man!" she shouted. "You'll not be taking food from the family to feed that stray cat!"

"No, Mom," I answered and then bolted with the bowl of milk. Back outside, I placed it underneath the porch. To my relief, Stella was still there in the box and lying on the soft rags.

I went to bed thinking of the beauty and wonder of that little animal. It was my hope that she would be a great companion through the coming years, and that we would be fast friends.

Going to sleep that night, I once again had the recurring dream of wandering in the nearby forests, of trout fishing and catching big, fat trout...but then, Stella appeared, scampering across the grass and coming toward me as I held up a stringer of newly caught fish.

I awoke especially early in the morning, dressed, and ran downstairs to check on my new friend. She was there in the box sleeping, and when I came near, she awoke and jumped out. Back in the kitchen, I put a bit of milk in a bowl and again managed to give it to Stella without being caught. For the rest of the many years I had this cat, not once did Mother allow the luxury of buying cat food. Either Stella ate scraps or caught her own food. No cat was going to add to the family expenses. Even now, I wonder if that was the case with many families in the fifties who struggled to meet the bills.

When finished with the milk, Stella scampered out on the grass. I lay down on the lawn, and when she came near, I petted her soft, furry head. Stretching contentedly, she nudged her head into my hand, begging me to continue.

But, the serenity was broken when a grasshopper flew in from the nearby open field. Seeing the insect, Stella stiffened, crouched low, crept forward, and pounced. The winged creature was caught in the cat's forepaws. Biting down, she devoured the head and then quickly crunched and consumed the rest.

Curious, I stood up and went into the field and caught another hopper from a tall blade of grass. I brought it back and turned it lose in front of my cat. Once again, she ate the head and then chewed up the rest. I repeated the process several times to make sure, and each time, no matter which end I gave her, she always managed to eat the head first and then the remainder. I was bewildered and proud. To my great astonishment, I discovered something I never thought possible. I had a grasshopper-eating cat. I mean, she seemed to really enjoy eating those hard-shelled things.

It was then that mother came out on the porch looking for me. "Charlie," she ordered. "Go in the house and eat your breakfast. Mind you, wash your hands. No telling what kind of germs that cat has." She looked at Stella in disgust. "You're not going to waste all day playing with that animal. Like I told you yesterday, I want you to start on the windows. You wash the inside ones today, and the outside tomorrow."

For once, I didn't complain; at least, Mother didn't tell me to get rid of the cat. I picked up Stella and put her back under the porch; but instinctively, I knew she wouldn't stay there during the day. I just hoped she would be safe until I could check up on her later.

After breakfast, I gathered a bucket, vinegar, a rag, and lots of old newspapers. Pouring vinegar into the pail, I ran the water until very hot and then filled the container half-full with it. As I cleaned the inside living room window, Mother came to check on my work. Washing down the glass with the wet rag, I then wadded up a page of the paper and began rubbing the pane dry. The window from the inside looked cleaner, but the outside still showed dust and rain spots.

Mother went into the kitchen to do dishes without making a comment. I knew what she was thinking. *Idle hands are the devil's workshop.*

Long ago, Mother declared war on dirt—and nearly won. Our big old Victorian house was immaculate on the inside, no dust, no dirt, and everything had its place. Mother stood over the interior like a commander on a ship—and woe to anyone who defied her orders.

Sighing, I knew that poor Stella would never be able to stay in the house. At least, for the moment, the cat was allowed to live under the porch, and for that, I was thankful. Somehow, I would have to sneak her food and milk whenever I could.

The rest of the summer slipped by quickly. Despite my many chores, I did take the time to read books, play with Stella, and go fishing. I never once missed the Saturday afternoon matinee at the movie theatre. At first, I had to be careful that my pet did not follow me when I left the house, but after a time, she developed her own routine and disappeared into the field to hunt or visit places that I would never know about.

By the end of summer, with my help, Stella grew and became sleek and healthy. A far cry from the pitiful skinny little thing she once was when she first came to our back door. I was so glad she found us, and that Mother had at least allowed me to keep her.

The summer ended and school bells rang. Still, Stella was part of my morning ritual. Mother insisted I eat breakfast first thing, make my bed, and pick up my room. After that, I would grab my books and head out the door. Stella always greeted me on the porch. We would horse around a bit before I petted her and told her to stay home as I started my long walk to school. But, to my great worry, like most cats, she did what she wanted. Usually, she found something else that interested her, and would turn back about a block from our house.

Winter came, and with it, the first snowfall. I worried about my cat and I tried to improve her home. I nailed a thick cloth over the entrance to the crawl space, made a better box for her, and put in heavier clean rags. To my relief, no matter how cold it got, Stella seemed no worse for wear.

Every day, Stella would scratch at the door, begging for food, and when Mother was not around, I would sneak my cat inside and feed her. Eventually, Mother would catch us, and demand I take her out. There were many other special evenings, or Saturdays or Sundays when I would hide Stella inside my sweater and sneak her inside where, for as much as an hour or more, we would hide behind the big couch. Together, we would snuggle next to the warm steam register, Stella curled up sleeping, and me reading an ever-present book.

Mother would eventually discover us and demand I remove the cat. Over and over again during those next five years that we lived in that house, I tried my best to sneak Stella inside. And, each time, with stolid determination, Mother scolded me and out Stella would go. This was an ever-constant struggle of wills between my mother and me, all through my childhood.

As the years passed, Mother seemed to come around to my Stella. More than once, I caught her calling for the cat from the back porch and feeding her bits of food from that night's supper.

Then one summer, to my great surprise, she brought the cat in a box up to my bedroom. Stella was heavy and broad, pregnant with kittens and looking miserable. Together, mother and I sat on the edge of the bed, along with my younger brother, and watched kittens be born.

"Pay attention," said Mother, "and you'll learn something. Both of you were born in a similar manner." Come to think on it, I believe that was the closest Mother came to having a 'birds and bees' talk with us.

I remember my brother's eyes, big and round—and I must admit, it was a miraculous thing to watch. It was up to me to care for the kittens that were promptly moved back to the only acceptable place for animals— under the porch. And, when they were old enough, I was the one who had to find homes for them.

Then, in the spring of my thirteenth year, Mother announced that they had sold our house to my dad's sister and her husband, and that we were moving to a bigger one on the other side of town. I remember coming home on the last day of school in June and finding the house open and empty. Every stick of furniture and every item we owned was gone, taken away by the movers. My brother was there, wandering from room to room, mouth open, in awe of how vastly different the old house looked. The emptiness gave it an eerie and forlorn appearance. Such a change in our lives was hugely disturbing.

Both of us took one long last look around and reluctantly left—but not before I found a cardboard box. Capturing Stella against her crying wishes, I stuffed her inside and shut the top lids.

My brother and I walked across town, he carrying my books and I the box with my precious cat. There was a garage at the new house and I locked Stella in. Then, I took a quick look through our home, noting my bedroom and that my possessions were safely ensconced.

After a time, I grabbed my bicycle and rode downtown to the library. There, I pored over the few books about cats. I finally read an article that said if a cat is moved and kept locked up for two weeks it would forget its past and become acclimated to the new environment. Relieved, I went home, hopeful that Stella would like living in the garage.

It appeared the article I found was not factual—at least, not for *my* cat. Keeping her locked up for two weeks in the garage did not work. Despite my visiting her several times a day and giving her food, at every opportunity she tried to escape. And then, at the end of the second week, she did.

After a day of searching, I returned to our old neighborhood and found Stella, back in her place under the porch. Twice more, I took her back to the garage, and both times, after a two-week stay, she managed to slip past me and escape. I felt so bad that my cat would not stay with me at our new residence. How I would miss her. I went back to be with her one more time.

Uncle Benjamin who had purchased the house was standing on the porch and watching me look into the crawl space underneath.

"Won't stay put, will she?" he asked.

"No," I said.

"She's not under there," said my uncle, pointing. "Don't worry. I'll take care of her. I like cats. Here's a bag of food I bought for her. Perhaps you would like to go inside and feed her while you're here?"

To my astonishment, my uncle opened the porch door. I walked through the house into the living room. There I saw my Stella curled up comfortably in a sunny spot on the couch. I felt both happy and sad as I made my way home that afternoon.

So ended my long relationship with Stella—the one animal that had meant so much to me. Looking back at those five years together, now some fifty-eight years ago, I remember with great fondness my beautiful cat and all she meant to me. My intervention helped my cat survive and reach her life potential. I know that living with my uncle, Stella became fat and happy and lived to a ripe old age.

As for what Stella did for me...she gave a lonely little boy friendship and comfort. She taught me the importance of caring for someone or something other than myself. And...I suppose, this is the reason that I have always shared my home with one or more cats.

About the Author—Charlie Steel

Charlie Steel, Tale-Weaver Extraordinaire, is a novelist and internationally published author of short stories. Steel credits the catalyst for his numerous books and hundreds of short stories to be the result of being a voracious reader, along with having worked at many varied and assorted occupations. Some of his experiences include service in the Army, labor in the oil fields, in construction, in a foundry, and as a salvage diver. Early in his life he was recruited by the US Government and spent five years behind the Iron Curtain. Steel's work has been recognized and reviewed by various publications and organizations including *Publisher's Weekly*, Western Fictioneers, and Western Writers of America. Steel holds five degrees including a PhD. He continues to read, research, and collect western literature. Steel lives on an isolated ranch at the base of Greenhorn Mountain, in Southern Colorado. (www.charliesteel.net)

Pollyanna

C.J. Samuels

I grew up in a house as the youngest of nine children. Our home was always full—my parents seemed to adopt in strays, people and animals. The difference was that the animals always stayed outside.

Herbie the goose, Leanda the cat, our dogs Pickles and Diamond Jim, and Babby the sheep—who kept breaking the screen door because she wanted in the house with my sisters—were all part of our menagerie.

My mother had a strict rule about animals in her house. We had a barn when I was small, and she faithfully made sure they were warm inside it. When we moved, we had a garage, and if the weather was severe, she would allow the dogs in the basement.

She had a fear of finding an animal hair in her food. Potlucks made her nervous, because she wouldn't eat from a home that had an inside cat. She was paranoid that someone would allow a cat on their table or counter. She actually gagged thinking about it.

As Mom aged, she lost her ability to walk due to a neuromuscular disorder. Her eyesight and hearing failed. Dementia took over, and we only saw glimpses of the mother we used to know. She spent most of her time in a blue recliner in the living room of my parents' home.

When her grandchildren visited, Mom allowed them to bring their dogs in—probably because she could no longer walk outside to see them—and she truly did love animals. She would still remind the kids never to allow any animal in their kitchen.

It was close to Thanksgiving in 2008 when Dad was outside in the barn. Winter came early that year, with snow already blowing. He heard a small animal under his tractor, but he couldn't see what it was. He told me he thought he was going to have to set a live trap to catch it. He did go a couple of more times that day to check on it. He set some food nearby, hoping it would come out. As he kept checking, the food was disappearing but the animal wouldn't show itself if Dad was near.

It took three full days until Dad finally coaxed out the nuisance. A small, frightened, very skinny, and extremely dirty dachshund came creeping toward him. Dad brought her in the house and we tried to hide her from Mom. I sneaked the poor little dog into the bathroom and warmed her up. She was so grateful, and stayed quiet. I had her in the bathtub trying to clean her up and when we were done, she barked. That was it. Mom heard it.

"What was that?" I heard Mom say. "Sounded like a dog...bring it in here."

My heart sank.

Dad opened the door and said, "If she's dried off, bring her on in the living room and show your mom."

Mom's eyes were full of cataracts, but they lit up like I hadn't seen happen in years when I brought the little dachshund in.

"Well, that's my Pollyanna!" she exclaimed. "Bring her here."

Dad and I stared at each other. Sure, Mom had dementia, but neither of us could believe she had forgotten how she felt about dogs in the house.

Mom was lying with a blanket over her in the recliner. I laid "Pollyanna" between her feet. The little dog curled up like she knew exactly where she belonged. Mom sat and talked to her. She decided to call her Polly, for short. Before long, both of them were sleeping contently.

While they napped, I called the Humane Society and the dog warden, and left dad's name and number. I called several neighbors. No one had lost a dachshund, and none of the neighbors knew anyone that had one.

That night, we got Mom ready for bed. She had little movement in her legs. We had to lift her from her recliner, put her in her wheelchair, make a bathroom visit and then get her into her nightgown and wheel her again into the bedroom. It was a process every night. Mom insisted on sleeping in her own bed. She said she had been sleeping beside dad for over fifty years and it wasn't going to change now.

Polly followed mom the entire time, staying away from the wheels.

It only took a few minutes before the dog started crying and whining for Mom. I heard words that night I would have sworn I would never hear my mother utter.

"Put her up here."

I looked at Dad and he shrugged. I put her up on the bed with Mom, and Polly snuggled on a pillow beside Mom's head. Polly had found her sleeping place. The next night, there were *three* pillows on the bed. Polly's was in the middle, and she adjusted it each night until it fit her perfectly.

Dad took her to the vet, who said she was healthy and already spayed. He updated her shots, just in case.

Over the next couple of weeks, we kept warning Mom that Polly might have an owner that missed her. Mom ignored every word we said. Polly was *hers*—and she knew it!

It became clear, quickly, who was now running the house. Polly was in charge of barking when the doorbell rang, always on alert. She had full run of the house, including the kitchen. If Dad was cooking, she was in the kitchen; after all, there could be *meat* involved! Her dog dishes were in the kitchen beside the table. Visitors were required to pet her and to tell Mom how pretty and smart her little dog was.

It was bound to happen eventually. Polly got into something she shouldn't have, and Dad yelled at her. Immediately, my mother was furious—and it *wasn't* at Polly. Mercy did not rain from the recliner. Polly ran to Mom's chair and took her usual spot. That was the moment that the "evil eye" was developed. Mom and her dog laid in the recliner, both giving the same look to Dad. Forgiveness did not come quickly. Mom trusted Dad with her nine children and all the grandchildren—her dog was a different story.

Over the next two years, everyone developed their own relationship with Polly. Belly rubs were given by all the grandchildren who came in. Two of my sisters and I adored her. The other two, not so much. They were very good to Polly, just not inclined to take orders from her when she laid at their feet and demanded something. They received the "evil eye" on a regular basis. My dad called Polly our "sister."

When Mom's health failed, Polly guarded her. I had never heard her growl until then. She parked herself beside her owner, and if she didn't know and trust you, you weren't getting close.

Mom's passing changed the relationship between Polly and Dad. Dad was never alone. He started taking her in the car with him. She was more demanding than ever, mostly because Dad did what she asked. Polly started putting on weight because Dad loved cookies—and he always shared them. She turned up her nose at dog cookies.

I kept her a couple of times for Dad when he went to church camp. Her behavior didn't change from his house to mine. Polly was the ultimate in spoiled dogs. She got along well with my dogs, and each time she stayed, she seemed comfortable. But when I took her home, Dad got the evil eye on arrival. Of course, he promptly gave her cookies to receive forgiveness.

Early in 2014, we found out dad had colon cancer. After his second surgery, he said he couldn't take care of Polly. She was overweight, and he couldn't take her outside as often as necessary. He told my sisters first that he knew I would take her—but any of us would have.

The day I picked her up, she went with me willingly. I told Dad I would bring her back on the day he asked. I took her little bed, her dishes, and the food he sent with her. I looked her over and trimmed her nails. No one was ever sure exactly how old our Polly was, but her cloudy blue eyes were showing some age.

Polly was also, at this point, very overweight and I refused to allow her any "people food." I have no back steps at my house, just a slight bump she had to get over to get to go outside. She would go to the back door and stare at me, hoping I would carry her out. I didn't—and I cried many times at that door. She would waddle herself outside by following my two dogs.

It only took a week or so, though, and she had lost enough weight chasing Sam, my bulldog, and Lucy, my chiweenie, that she could go outside with no problem. She figured out quickly that she got a low-fat meat dog treat each time she came in.

She rejected the dog food Dad sent, choosing instead to eat the food my dogs ate. She still begged for "people food," but finally resigned herself to dog food.

The exercise and diet worked. Polly lost enough weight that when my brother-in-law stopped at my house, he accused me of switching dogs—until she gave him the evil eye for not rubbing her belly. He knew right away that was Mom's dog.

She didn't lose the attitude she had always had. I warned my husband over and over. One day, I heard the dreaded words, "bad dog." Polly immediately ran to me for protection. A few hours later, my husband yelled again. He had picked his shoes up to put them on for work. Polly ran straight to him and sat at his feet. No protection needed this time, as she was proving a point. She had pooped in *both* his shoes and just sat there giving him her evil eye. Never again did anyone say "bad dog" to her.

On a Tuesday in August, 2014 Dad had his last chemo treatment. We were all relieved that he had beat cancer. The joy did not last. I stopped at his house on Friday of that week, hugged and kissed him goodbye for what I had no idea would be the last time. Forty minutes later, my sister called and told me to come to the emergency room. My strong father, my rock, had collapsed with an aneurysm. He made his way to his heavenly home on Labor Day.

I still had Polly. She was still losing weight, and more active all the time—and she was a joy. I felt like I still had a piece of Mom and Dad, and she needed me. I sent pictures and videos to my family members. I believe they all felt the connection that I did.

At the beginning of October, Polly woke up one morning and couldn't walk. She didn't seem to be in pain. I immediately took her to the vet, who thought she had a dislocated disc in her back. He gave me steroids with stern advice that they might not work. With Polly's age and history, all we could do was hope and pray. I took her back to the vet a couple of days later with no change. He upped the prescription he had given her and told me I would need to make a decision.

A few days later, I heard a noise in the bedroom. Polly was under the bed having a seizure. I had to roll her in a blanket to get her out. She didn't recognize me. I called the only person I thought would be home at that time of day: my brother-in-law, Tom. He said he would meet me at the vet's.

Polly calmed down as I tried to quit crying. I could see Tom's truck when I pulled into the parking lot. I sobbed as I carried in a very still Polly. Doc looked at her and told me it was time. She was in pain, and her life was over. Her little body just hadn't figured that out yet.

I talked to her and petted her as they gave her the initial shot. She finally relaxed and slept. He allowed me to have a few minutes with her, and then Polly went across the Rainbow Bridge to join Mom and Dad.

I cried. I sobbed. I threw up. In that moment, I suppose I grieved the loss of my parents that I hadn't been able to give in to before.

I contacted the people who had bought my parents' house, and they graciously allowed us to bury Polly there. It was where she belonged.

It took a few hours until the date hit me—October 16th—*Dad's birthday.*

Who would have imagined a scraggly little stray would affect so many lives? I didn't. I'm sure my family didn't. Mom told us Polly was an angel. I think that could be true. I don't think it was a coincidence that she appeared in the barn when Mom was so sick. I don't think the date she passed was a coincidence. Polly was only on loan to us. Mom and Dad needed her. *I* needed her. The joy she brought with her smiles, her "happy dog dance" that appeared in videos, and yes, even her "evil eye" look had to be heaven-sent.

Today, I still have Sammie, Lucy, and Lucky—all rescues. Rescue animals are the best pets, so loving and so grateful to find a safe home that loves them back! The shelters are always full, and you may just find the love of your life in a cage there, waiting for a miracle—just as our bundle of love was waiting, under a tractor, in my parents' barn.

About the Author—C.J. Samuels

C.J. Samuels was born and raised in rural Ohio. After more than twenty years working in service at an auto dealership, she picked up the proverbial pen and began writing, thanks to a lot of encouragement from her family and friends.

C.J. always has a pot of coffee on, and a welcoming chair for anyone who needs to talk. C.J. was the daughter of the local preacher and had three kids of her own. From attorney, to finished construction builder, to a Marine, C.J.'s kids are her pride and joy. C.J. has many "adopted" extra family members, including ten grandchildren that she claims as her own, along with her newest grandchild born in May 2016.

C.J. is a born and bred Buckeye fan. She has three rescue dogs; an English bulldog named Sammie, a chi-weenie named Lucy, and a beagle mix named Lucky.

In each of her books, you will find stories from her family history. In her eyes, family is most important.

The Love of a Cat

Jim Landwehr

Our family pet stories are mostly sordid tales of love turned tragic, but they are also a product of how my family rolled in the seventies. We were six kids being raised by my single-parent mother who worked full time at a hospital collection agency in downtown St. Paul, Minnesota.

Amongst the six of us, someone was always bringing in a stray cat or a "freebie" dog from a friend. We loved our pets, but because of their typically short residencies, our emotional attachments grew more superficial as pets came and went. There seemed to be no sense in getting too emotionally involved to an adopted stray tomcat or mutt, as most tended to be runners and drifters—hobo pets.

Over time, we began to understand that they were likely only passing through with a short stay at our house on their way to another home or, worse, an untimely death.

Tonto showed up on our doorstep one day, and after a feeding or two, decided we were okay and became a part of our family. He was a good-looking, large gray cat with a healthy coat giving him the look of a Chartreux, or maybe a Russian Blue. Tonto took the place of Sam, another gray cat we took in who decided life on the road was better than life in a house with six kids. So, this was our period where gray cats were our thing, for whatever reason.

Somehow, Tonto was assigned the name of the Native American, politically incorrect sidekick to the Lone Ranger. It didn't really fit his nature as a big old tomcat, but the silliness of the name kind of grew on us over time. After a couple of years of calling him by it, we couldn't really picture him with a name any different. One might say it was a better choice than Fat Cat, a highly unimaginative moniker given to another gray feline of ours from a few years earlier. Tonto was nothing if not unique.

Tonto had a thing for the ladies to accompany his reputation as a fighter. There were several occasions where we let him out at night and didn't see him for several days. During some of the longer stretches, we actually put his food dish away, thinking he was gone forever. Then, one day, he would show up unannounced at the back door, meowing and looking up at us like we were stupid. We'd stand there with our mouths agape, and he'd just look at us as if to say, "Well, what are you looking at? Are you gonna let me in or not?"

Like most of our cats, he made sure to cash in on all of his nine lives.

On one occasion, Tonto had been on the losing side of a fight and had a nasty open gash on his side. Mom guessed he might have been in a scrap with a raccoon or a faster, stronger cat. After a day or so, the wound was pus-covered and not healing well, so she decided that he should be checked out by the vet. My younger brother Rob and I were tasked with taking him to the veterinarian.

Because Mom was not home, we didn't have her car to transport the cat. With a bit of reluctance and a cautionary lecture, Tom offered to let us use his recently purchased Chevy LUV (Light Utility Vehicle) pickup for the job. The LUV was a small pickup truck, with a fire engine red paint job and a white topper over the bed in back. Tom loved his new truck and regularly reminded us so. Rob, a newly licensed driver, piped up that he wanted to drive the truck to the vet.

Conceding to his enthusiasm, yet wanting to drive the new vehicle myself, I said, "Fine, but I get to drive on the way back."

It was a battle of wills to corral the cat. Rob and I chased Tonto from room to room trying to capture him. After a ten-minute chase-down, we eventually cornered Tonto. For reasons unknown, we did not own a pet carrier at the time. Using our best teenage innovation, we used a cardboard box covered by a towel—an animal carrier abomination, to be sure—but it was all we had to work with.

Rob and I figured that it would work out just fine. After all, we were the pet owners, and our ailing cat would surely submit willingly to our captivity and subsequent medical treatment.

I was charged with cat duty and took my place in the front passenger seat, boxed cat in my lap, while Rob slid behind the wheel of the LUV. Because these were the days before seatbelts were mandatory, neither of us buckled up. The vet was a short three-mile trip, so no big deal. What could possibly go wrong?

As we crept past the first few houses, Tonto, sensing some inherent weaknesses in his makeshift cat jail, began to work his way out. His sharp claws poked through the towel and scratched at my hand. I tried to stretch the towel tighter with little success. It seemed like every time I got a paw pushed back in, another one appeared from a different gap. No doubt, Tonto and his claws had the upper hand in this fight.

As the LUV moved up the block, gaining speed, Tonto became more and more agitated. He started to work his head and upper torso through the gap between the towel and the side of the box. My efforts were largely in vain, as Tonto swiftly maneuvered out and into my lap and chest.

At the end of the block, Rob took a right turn and started giggling at the antics of the cat and my attempts to pry his claws off of me and stuff him back in the box. He slipped through my hands and moved onto Rob's arm and shoulder with claws extended to emphasize his discontent.

Rob's attention turned strictly to the now free-roaming, frantic cat. He swatted at Tonto, and inadvertently began to accelerate as the truck began drifting to the right. In the midst of the chaos in the cab, I looked up to see us heading toward a parked car.

"Look out!" I shouted.

Then, *wham!*

The truck slammed the car with such force that it was pushed into a third vehicle parked in front of it. Rob and I did our best crash-test dummy impersonations as our little truck crunched, recoiled and spun out into the middle of the intersection. My head hit the windshield with a thump, and I saw stars.

The engine revved and howled, screaming a racket like spoons in a garbage disposal. I shook my head, then looked over at Rob. He was knocked out cold and bleeding from his top lip after apparently hitting the steering wheel.

After I regained my wits, I tried shaking Rob into consciousness. "Rob. Rob, are you alright?" I reached over and shut off the sputtering engine. After a few seconds, he slowly opened his eyes and came to.

He looked at me and, upon realizing what had happened, said, "Ugh! Tom's going to kill me."

The first thing I could think of to say at the time was, "It's okay, I'll go get him. You stay here." In hindsight, I realized that was like me saying, "Let me go get him so he can kill you."

I opened the door, and Tonto scrambled out of the cab with cat-like indifference to our condition. I staggered into the street and down the block toward home. I kept thinking, *Wow, are we going to be in trouble when Tom hears about this.* I walked in the door and saw Tom sitting on the sofa. "What are you doing home?" he said

"We got in an accident!"

"An accident? Where?" Tom asked in disbelief

"At the end of the block."

"Are you guys okay?" Tom asked, more concerned about us than his new truck.

"Yeah, I just bumped my head. Rob was knocked out, but he's conscious now."

Tom and I ran up the block to the scene. Rob stood outside the truck. Tom checked with Rob to see if he was okay. Rob nodded remorsefully.

Tom was clearly shocked at how badly his truck was damaged. The force of the impact had pushed the radiator fan against the grill so the fan would no longer spin, even if the truck was in running condition. The right front fender and hood were badly crumpled. After we had finished with it, there wasn't much to love about this LUV.

Fortunately, neither Rob nor I was badly hurt in the crash. Tom and Mom both had good insurance, and after a few long weeks, his truck was restored to near-new condition. He did have to live without his truck during the peak of hunting season, a fact he reminded us of repeatedly over the years. Hunting was why he bought the truck in the first place. To his credit though, I still remember his first reaction was to the safety and welfare of Rob and me.

Three days after the crash, as my mother was leaving for work, Tonto was waiting at the front door. He'd come back like the prodigal cat. His wound scabbed over quite nicely in that time since his near-death experience. Mom let him in the door as she muttered, "Stupid cat," and continued on her way to work.

Tonto went on to live as a family pet for many years thereafter. He did contract some sort of ear infection that caused his ears to lop. We still loved him, but it was a little harder to look at him without smiling and feeling a bit sorry for him.

Some might look at our transient pet fostering as neglectful. I prefer to look at it as giving a second chance to an animal whose fate was day-to-day anyway. We did the best we could, given the gypsy nature of these animals. We showed them love and affection, gave them food and shelter, and yet, sometimes they still chose life on the road.

They each played a role in shaping our family, some as foster pets, some as long-time residents. One thing is sure: Tonto certainly left his mark on our family folklore.

And all it took was a little LUV.

About the Author—Jim Landwehr

Jim Landwehr has two poetry collections, *Reciting from Memory*, by Underground Voices, and *Written Life* by eLectio Publishing. His first book, *Dirty Shirt: A Boundary Waters Memoir*, was published by eLectio Publishing in 2014. He has non-fiction stories published in *Main Street Rag, Prairie Rose Publications' Memories From Maple Street, U.S.A.—Leaving Childhood Behind and Memories From Maple Street, U.S.A.—The Best Christmas Ever, Steam Ticket*, and others. His poetry has been featured in *Torrid Literature Journal, Every Day Poems, Off the Coast Poetry Journal*, and many others. He enjoys fishing, kayaking, biking and camping with his kids in the remote regions of Wisconsin and Minnesota. For more, visit: www.jimlandwehr.com

I'd Trade My Life for Annie's

Cher'ley Grogg

Eight chubby puppies ran around sniffing and falling all over each other. The mother hovered close by; the father lounged on the living room rug, and the grandfather peeked from a room down the hall. The pups all looked alike, but one broke free of the pack and ran over to me. She pawed at my ankles for attention. This was the one. I picked her up. The mother came to see what I was doing with her pup, but she was quickly called away by the seven other yelping whelps.

I was so excited! It had been thirteen years since I'd

picked out a puppy. Zacchaeus, our little seven-pound Pomeranian, was getting old. Del and I had talked about getting another dog, but we never had the room. We were "big dog" people, but the places we had lived weren't right to have a big dog. Now, we'd bought this larger home, so we had the room to be a two-dog family.

We were on vacation when I found the ad in a local paper about Great Danes for sale. We went to look them over and fell in love with the little black pup. She wasn't entirely black—she had a red cast to her fur. She was a dark reverse brindle, which confused people, because it was an unusual color.

As a registered dog, we wanted her to have a royal name, yet one that would also have a personal name for us. Since she belonged to us, we gave her our name—Grogg. Her parents were Kings and Queens, so we called her Grogg's Princess Roxanne. "Roxanne" was the name my husband had kidded around about naming our granddaughter. Her call name would be "Annie."

She loved being close to us. We taught her to fetch the first day, and she was housebroken by day three. We were staying in a campground, so she got lots of attention from the families there, as well as the grounds keepers. She drew attention wherever we went.

Finally, it was time to go home. We were excited to show off the newest member of our family. Zack loved her. He got a renewed vitality as he romped with her. She was already bigger than he was. Then our children came to visit, and brought the grandchildren. She romped and played with them; tug-of-war was a favorite game. I knew when she was winning, because there would be shrieks of pain from the grandkids when those sharp little puppy teeth would make contact.

Once she got tired, she'd cuddle up with someone and nap. She did a lot of eating and napping as she grew larger and larger. She finally reached a height where our youngest grandchild, who had just started walking, could walk under her.

Obedience training was a walk in the park for her. She learned all the commands easily, and we practiced each new command over and over until she became bored. She got to be around a lot of different people and other animals almost daily as I walked her in the city park.

Before the classes had ended, I had her in the country, visiting my daughter. We were standing out by the barn talking and looking at the horses. All of a sudden, one of the horses neighed. This scared her, and she took off at a fast trot of her own. The only handicap she had was dragging me along behind her. I finally got to my feet, but I had four broken fingers where her leash had been intertwined between them.

My husband had to finish her training.

The last night of classes rolled around, and I watched as my husband put her through her paces. "Stay, Annie, stay." My husband gave her the strict command. She had done so well; my chest swelled as I watched her complete task after task. I glanced at the other dogs and their masters, but laughter brought my attention back to Annie and Del. There Annie was, crawling as quickly as she could across the middle of the floor. She stopped right in front of him and looked up so lovingly that it melted my heart.

The teacher held the big trophy up in the air. "One of the dogs here did an astounding job, but failed in one command, so that knocked her out of the running. Too bad she loved her master so much she couldn't stand the separation from him." The teacher gave a loud laugh, and then he announced the winner of the trophy—but Annie was still *our* winner.

My husband and I are truck drivers, and she quickly adapted to the trucking life. She would sit beside me while I drove, and periodically, she'd lay her chin on my thigh. This was her way of giving me a hug, and a way to get a few extra pats on her head.

She loved to sleep with us. It didn't matter that the bunk was only the size of a twin bed, with two adult people already in it! Sometimes, Del would say, "Off." She'd reluctantly climb out of bed. Little did he know, she sat there and waited for him to go back to sleep, and then she'd stand on the bed with her front legs. She'd bounce the bed. "Annie off!" She'd lie back down. A little later, she would be back to do it again. When he didn't say anything, she jumped over his legs and onto the back of the bed. I would just move my legs over and giggle to myself so that I wouldn't wake him.

There was one big thing we had a problem with her doing. Annie always let us know when she had to relieve herself, but every once in awhile, she'd get something that didn't agree with her. It usually hit her while we were out of the truck. Upon our return, we'd see her through the windshield, jumping from the driver's seat to the passenger seat. When she couldn't take it anymore, she would chomp the microphone cord from the CB radio. As she streaked out of the cab, I would notice the mic was missing. I laughed and said, "I guess she was calling someone who cared."

We decided to take a month off one summer, so we'd have time to camp out on our houseboat. It was a big v-bottomed, steel, 32-foot houseboat. My husband was very careful with it, never getting in too close to shore, unless he knew the area. We sure didn't want to get a hole in the bottom.

One day, we were cruising down the Ohio River. Del said, "You better keep an eye on Annie."

"She's taller than the chains. I don't think we—"

There was a loud splash. He killed the engine. I ran out onto the deck. There she was, trying to swim to the boat. She finally made it. We tried different ways to lift her up, but nothing seemed to be working. I jumped into the water and pushed as Del pulled on her, but there was no way of doing it without hurting her. I looked to the left at the West Virginia side of the river; then I looked to the right at the Ohio side. Ohio seemed closer. I grabbed her collar and started swimming, dragging her behind me.

Suddenly, I hit a strong under-current. I couldn't get anywhere, and neither could she. She got scared and jumped on top of me, pushing me under her.

Del was afraid of getting too close and running the risk of sucking us under the boat. He tried throwing a rope, but I couldn't reach it, and I couldn't pull her and myself any farther out or back in toward the shore. We were just stuck. I was exhausted. He was pulling the rope back up.

I started crying, "Please, don't pull it back, please."

"Honey, I'm throwing it back. Let the dog go."

"I can't."

"Let her go. I can get another dog; I can't get another you."

I whispered, "I can't." With all my strength, I pulled Annie forward, and then I pulled myself a little farther. Finally, we got out of the current. Del had started the boat again and had run it straight into the bank, no thoughts or worries about the damage that might happen to it. He was coming out after us. I told him we were okay. I could touch bottom, so I knew Annie could, too.

We got her back on the boat and in the cabin. We closed the doors as we went back to our campsite. Over the next few weeks, she learned to swim a little better, but she still couldn't get out very far without needing help to get back in.

Zack, the Pom, had no desire to be in the water, so all the while we had our adventure on the wild seas—or so I thought of the river after that—Zack lay on a rug in the galley.

Two things I knew that day. One: all dogs can't naturally swim; and two: I'd gladly give my life for my dog.

Zack passed on that November. It was hard, but he was old, and it was his time. Annie seemed to understand, and she comforted us as best she could.

After Annie had crossed the rainbow bridge, I mourned for her. I spent many nights in tears, and my mind filled with thoughts of her. One evening, as I was driving along in our eighteen-wheeler, I felt her head rest on my thigh. I reached down to touch her, but she wasn't there. This happened a few more times, but I didn't reach for her, I just enjoyed the gentle pressure her head made as I drove down the road. Periodically, this happened again and again until we got another fur baby—Lizzie, a boxer pup. It happened one more time while Del and Lizzie slept soundly in the sleeper.

Then, I never felt my Annie again. I think she understood her job was finally done, and she could rest.

About the Author—Cher'ley Grogg

Cher'ley has written *The Journey Back—One Joy at a Time*, a devotional book. Her story, *Stamp Out Murder* is a cozy mystery set deep in the mountains of West Virginia, and *The Secret in Grandma's Trunk* is a YA novel featuring a spunky grandmother and a rebellious youth. Cher'ley is featured in *Small Town America* and *West Virginia Memories*. She contributed to the anthologies *Boys Will Be Boys, It's All About the Girls,* and the Prairie Rose Publications anthology *Cowboys, Creatures, and Calico*. She drives an eighteen-wheeler, loves the Lord, her husband, children, grandchildren, great-grandchildren, and her Cairn Terrier, Tootsie.

Goggies from Gog

Beverly Wells

As far back as I can remember when I was but as big as a widget, dogs simply made me smile. Yep, a picture, a store-bought soft stuffed one, a living, breathing dog—big or small—it didn't matter.

From what my parents told me, *one* of my first words was "goggie." They also said no matter where I was, looking out the window, in the car or stroller, at some gathering, in a restaurant, each and every time I saw a dog, I'd swing my legs, flay my arms, giggle and yell, "Here goggie! Here goggie!"

At the time, we lived with my granny in a two-family apartment house in Rhode Island where I was born, so we couldn't have a dog yet. I contented myself with enjoying the neighbors' dogs—or any dog I saw coming my way. I had oodles of stuffed dogs I dragged everywhere I went, and of course they slept with me, under me, over me and in my arms. I was surrounded by puppy love each naptime and every night. It was sheer heaven, and my heart overflowed with contentment.

When people asked, "Oh, sweetie, where did you get that pretty little dog?" I'd hug it tight and say, "Goggie from Gog." Granny, my parents, aunts, and uncles all said it was a running joke. By age three, I believe I finally articulated *doggie* and *God*.

We moved when I was five, and once settled in our new home, we got our first dog just after I turned six. My dad had always wanted his own hunting dog—an English setter. He'd only have one dog at a time so he could focus on him and train him well.

Our first setter, Pal, was black and white. He became dad's pride and joy. Mine, as well. Although Dad called Pal his hunter, he was definitely our family's dog. More often than not, that spotted guy ran the neighborhood with me and my friends. When in the house, he was to stay in the back hall off the kitchen on his bed, but when my mother was at work in the evening, I'd hustle Pal into the living room. Placing my bed pillow on the carpeted living room floor, Pal and I would lie down to share my pillow as we cuddled and watched TV.

However, my mother had an eagle's eye for spotting dog hairs on the living room carpet. My dad would hide his smile as she bellowed down the walls. I just tried to block my ears. When it came to our dogs, my dad most assuredly became and stayed true to being my partner in crime. Bosom dog-loving buddies through thick and thin.

Our next English setter was named Jiggs. His coat appeared almost all white, but when you drew closer, you could see random, medium-sized golden-brown spots—sometimes called liver spots. He walked me to school every morning and then returned home. If I didn't have any activity after school, my mother would let him out in time for him to run to the school and walk me home. To and from, he always carried my books in a book strap. The school was about a mile away.

One year for St. Patrick's Day, while my dad was bowling with his league, my mother and I—yes, I talked her into it—mixed green food coloring in water and bathed Jiggs. He was the prettiest shade of a cross between lime and fern—a lovely light green, indeed. When my dad walked in the door, Jiggs lay on his bed sporting a dark-green derby hat, a felt shamrock bowtie, and a corncob pipe that he obediently—and most proudly—held hanging out of his mouth. I don't believe I'd ever heard my dad swear. And even then, the only thing he could manage to spit out through clenched teeth with his eyes round as saucers and skin blanched to chalk white was, *"What have you done to my hunter?"*

I held my breath until I thought I might explode. He silently and unhurriedly left the room. Only then did I dare a shallow breath while remaining silent and cautious. Dad turned the TV on and remained in the living room for what seemed to be hours. Most likely, it equaled only a few minutes.

Eventually, he reappeared in the kitchen and asked us how many baths did we think it would take before *"that green"* would be totally washed out? I breathed a sigh of relief as my dad shook his head, and I realized that familiar twinkle in his dark-brown eyes spoke forgiveness.

That next morning, Jiggs walked me to school. His green hadn't faded one bit, and he sported his green derby hat and shamrock bow tie, while the corn cob pipe dangled from the bow tie. He became the only dog that was ever allowed into the school by the principal, who couldn't stop laughing. Jiggs's picture also made the newspaper. One of the neighbors called to say he *knew* he hadn't been drinking hard stuff that morning, but...was our dog really *green*?

So, from day one that I noticed a dog, my heart was spoken for. My husband, sons, and I adopted Amber, who was part collie, then our other little girl, Velvet, who was part lab. Each lived to a ripe old age, and both were spoiled rotten. My husband used to jokingly say that he or she is "Just A Dog". I've always answered back, "There isn't such a thing as 'Just A Dog'." Maybe it's their loving eyes, their unconditional love and devotion, or their hearts connecting with mine each and every time I encounter one of them that makes me feel this way. Is it any wonder pawprints are stamped across my heart?

Over twelve years ago, we lost Velvet to cancer. Amber and Velvet had truly been part of our family, treasured loved ones. But it always takes a while for anyone to recover from the loss of their beloved animal, and my husband wasn't sure either one of us needed to experience another painful loss of a dog. Did we really need another dog now that we were soon heading toward retirement? No more rushing home to let the dog outside; we could stop and have dinner out. He made it sound sensible. Didn't he?

I lasted three months. I started going to the shelter to look at the dogs. I knew before I went the first time that I'd be getting another—sooner or later. It appeared it would be later as they'd had an outbreak of Parvo. They had accepted several litters of pups from down South after Katrina, and Parvo ran rampant throughout the facility. All the animals had been put under quarantine. But how would I tell my hubby I needed a sweet baby so desperately? Would he be hurt that he couldn't fill that aching, lonely gap in my heart? Would he be upset that I *wanted* to go back to racing home to the dog after work?

The problem took care of itself after several weeks of me worrying. Hubby found an older model Mustang he'd been wanting forever. Hmmm... So...he got his Mustang, and floated on cloud nine. That's when I said, "I've been waiting for the quarantine to lift, but...I want a dog." Of course, he agreed! With the quarantine lifted, I now planned to go and see if any dog appealed to me.

But before I had a chance to go back, I received a call from the shelter. They knew I was looking for a dog, and I'd just made the commitment that I'd start volunteering there. Also, I was contemplating being on the board. The dog warden and deputy sheriff had brought in two six-month-old brothers who had existed on a two-foot chain outside a trailer. They had been extensively beaten and abused by both people and other dogs. They also suffered from severe malnutrition—and the list went on.

It was Friday before the Memorial Day weekend, and both dogs needed more attention than the shelter could give them—they feared neither dog would survive throughout the weekend. Being a nurse and a devoted lover of dogs, I'm sure they knew I would take at least one of them. I rushed to the shelter—and fell in love with

Jamie. I named him right off the bat, as I was reading an Irish romance novel at the time. I loved him the moment I saw him. A man with an eight-year-old son had offered Jamie's brother a loving home, as well.

Jamie, part black lab and border collie, was more fearful than any dog I'd ever seen. He had the saddest eyes that pulled at my heartstrings. He was reluctant to even try the food we offered, too frightened that he'd be attacked. It took lots of gentle encouragement, and long hours of patience, since he became defensive when another dog or a person approached him.

Panicked, he'd leap across the room whenever hubby picked up the newspaper to read. It took almost two years before he became more trusting of others. Now, he has almost thirty doggie friends up and down the lake road he looks forward to seeing on our walks, allows bicyclists to pass without shuddering, and watches joggers go by without becoming wild. This now-seventy-pound sweet, loving boy has whittled his way into our hearts. He's the apple of my eye.

****

At the shelter, we send this in a sympathy card to anyone who has lost any four-legged family member. I totally am a believer. I hope you are, too.

Just this side of heaven is a place called Rainbow Bridge.

When an animal dies that has been especially close to someone here, that pet goes to Rainbow Bridge. There are meadows and hills for all of our special friends so they can run and play together. There is plenty of food, water and sunshine, and our friends are warm and comfortable.

All the animals who had been ill and old are restored to health and vigor. Those who were hurt or maimed are made whole and strong again, just as we remember them in our dreams of days and times gone by. The animals are happy and content, except for one small thing: They each miss someone very special to them, who had to be left behind.

They all run and play together, but the day comes when one suddenly stops and looks into the distance. His bright eyes are intent. His eager body quivers. Suddenly, he begins to run from the group, flying over the green grass, his legs carrying him faster and faster.

You have been spotted, and when you and your special friend finally meet, you cling together in joyous reunion, never to be parted again. The happy kisses rain upon your face; your hands again caress the beloved head, and you look once more into the trusting eyes of your pet, so long gone from your life, but never absent from your heart.

Then, you cross Rainbow Bridge together...

Author Unknown

About the Author—Beverly Wells

For years, Bev devoted her life to family and nursing. Once she read romance novels, she was hooked. Now, as an award-winning author, she writes humorous, sensuous (sweet to spicy) historical romance. Living in the Finger Lakes Region of New York State with her husband and rescued dog, Jamie, she enjoys volunteering at the shelter, NASCAR, flower gardening, swimming, boating, and cooking for friends and family. She adores her two granddaughters and, of course, chocolate. For more info, visit her author page on Prairie Rose Publications.com, her website, blog, Facebook as Bev Lewis or Beverly Wells, or email her at *beverlywellsauthor@gmail.com*.

Everything's Hunky Dory

Carol Huff

Before I got the truck and trailer out of the parking lot, my beloved miniature donkey, Pokeberry, had been given the lethal dosage of a barbiturate that stopped her loving heart. Tears flowed unheeded down my cheeks and dropped onto the leg of my jeans below. I was broken...numb...unaccepting.

No words can adequately draw a picture of how I felt as I headed back home that night with Pokeberry's nine-day old son, Hunky, behind me in the trailer. How would he accept his mother's death? He was a tiny boy, all alone in a massive world that was still new to him. Who would teach him the things babies need to learn from their mothers? Who would show him how to protect himself from predators? Or the proper way to eat? Or when to get in out of the weather? Who would teach him manners, and how to act in a herd? Who would point out to him how good it feels to roll in the mud after a spring rain?

As I watched the lights of the Veterinarian Campus disappear from my mirror, I carried all the blame for Pokeberry's death in my heart. *If I hadn't allowed her to be bred, this never would have happened. How selfish could I have been?*

As I drove back home, I had flashbacks to the time I first saw Pokeberry. She was an adorable gray and white spotted miniature donkey, thirty-three inches tall at the withers. I'd come to love the compact breed after a friend gave me my first one—a handsome boy named Jackson—as a pasture protector for my horses.

After researching the breed and realizing there was a big demand for them in the southeastern part of the country where I live, I decided to go into the business of raising and selling them. I don't know why I thought that, because I'd already tried raising dogs and never sold the first puppy after getting attached to them.

I went on a buying trip to find two jennies. As I looked over the herd, I immediately wanted them all. The farmer who owned them told me I shouldn't choose a donkey—I should let *them* pick *me.*

"Donkeys are the best judges of character. I won't sell you one unless he or she picks you."

"How will I know if one chooses me?"

"Just stand amongst them and you'll see. If none of

them pick you, then you'll have to go somewhere else to find one, because I always let my donkeys decide who they want to live with. They are the smartest animals in the world, and I trust their instincts more than I trust mine."

Fair enough. I entered the enclosure where a dozen of them scurried about.

The first donkey to approach was a red sorrel. She immediately sniffed my pockets for treats and wanted nothing more than to be petted and to have her long ears scratched. She seemed to think I hung the moon, and it didn't take me long to know she'd chosen me. I named her Rose.

I also wanted a gray-and-white one like the beauty in the corner who caught my eye. I got down on my knees to encourage her to look my way, but she refused.

Suddenly, I felt a nudge in my back as Pokeberry appeared out of nowhere. I saw her little white face streaked with purple juice from a pokeberry bush, and my heart fluttered. Her Cleopatra eyes looked directly into mine. She was a pretty girl, but not exactly what I was looking for. I preferred less white on her face, so I again focused my attention on the shy one in the corner. But when Pokeberry nudged me in the back again, I grinned. I knew she had picked me, and would join Rose in the trailer.

The two girls became inseparable. Many evenings, I pulled a lounge chair to the edge of the pasture and watched as they frolicked through the meadows, kicking up their heels.

Springtime is breeding season for donkeys. Because Rose and Pokeberry were only two years old, I wanted to wait another couple of years. Jackson, however, had other ideas, and I found him inside their enclosure one morning. He'd already completed his mission.

As the months passed and their bellies grew larger, a gnawing fear within me grew, too. *Pokeberry is so tiny—I hope she'll be okay. If she were in the wild, she'd be bred by now, so why are you worrying about it? Because she's not in the wild—she's your responsibility.*

On April Fool's Day of the next spring, Pokeberry went into hard, difficult labor. My heart sank once again. The baby's shoulders were stuck. I called my vet, who told me I needed to pull the baby when Pokeberry had her next contraction. Suddenly, I felt like Prissy in *Gone with the Wind*—I didn't know nuttin' 'bout birthin' donkeys.

I followed instructions, and pulled. Suddenly, the baby was on the floor of the stall. I cleared the bloody sac from his head as Pokeberry bit the umbilical cord. I breathed a sigh of relief!

Within a few minutes, the most gorgeous gray and white spotted baby I'd ever seen stood up on wobbly legs and began nursing. The downy fur on his forehead was snow white. I was immediately in love with the little guy. My heart sang! I couldn't have been any prouder than if I'd given birth to him myself.

"What a hunk you are, little one. The only name that suits you is Hunky!" I said out loud as I touched his silky white fur.

The next week passed quickly, and my fear over being irresponsible and letting the donkeys get bred too soon finally began to subside. Rose had not delivered yet, but I knew it would be any day now. She was larger than Pokeberry, so I didn't worry about her as much.

Hunky was learning all the things donkeys are supposed to under the tutelage of his mother. He spent long hours napping in the sun while Pokeberry grazed nearby. Then, he'd run circles around her before stopping in for a sip of milk. Fast circles. He looked like a NASCAR racer going around and around the track, with his mother waiting for him when he made a pit stop.

"Precious" doesn't adequately describe the bond they had. Pokeberry was a good mother. She would not allow him to get out of her sight, and she constantly "grunted" to let him know what he could and could not do.

The eighth day brought problems. As I made my feeding rounds that morning, I discovered that Pokeberry would not eat, not even peppermint candy, her favorite treat. She wouldn't drink, and refused to let Hunky nurse. I knew this was something pretty serious, so I called the vet. When he arrived, his examination revealed colic.

He ran a tube through her nose into her stomach, then pumped her full of mineral oil and water. Then, he gave her a shot for pain.

"Just imagine the worst upset stomach you've ever had and multiply it by ten. That's how she feels," the vet said.

"What about Hunky? He needs to eat and she won't let him near her."

"I've got a baby bottle with me. Get some goat milk for him until she's feeling better."

Eight hours and three bottles of goat milk later, Pokeberry was worse. I called the vet again. When he arrived, Pokeberry's head was hanging low, and her ears and mouth were ice cold. She shivered uncontrollably and was almost too weak to stand. She leaned into me, and I saw the pain in her sad eyes.

"She needs fluids, and lots of them. She needs an IV, but there's not a large-animal facility around here. My suggestion would be to take her to Athens to the University of Georgia Vet School. They're equipped to handle emergencies like this. I'll call and let them know you're coming."

"That's an hour away."

"Yes, but that's her only hope right now. She's got something worse than colic. Her lips are cold and her tongue is paralyzed. She can't swallow. She's had a stroke."

My heart sank.

"How can a donkey have a stroke?"

"Probably from the trauma of childbirth, if I had to guess. This whole thing has been too much for her."

The Veterinarian College had not been able to help my beloved Pokeberry. She couldn't swallow, and her breathing was labored. The paralysis, along with the colic, was too much for her and there was no hope. Her knees buckled and she fell into my lap as the vets examined her. Her big brown eyes begged me to help her, to get her out of that pain.

Crying uncontrollably after I'd been given the verdict, I kissed her goodbye and loaded Hunky into the trailer for the trip back home—without his mother. The vets thought it best if I got him out of there before they put Pokeberry to sleep. It was the hardest decision I ever had to make.

"This whole thing has been too much for her," kept replaying in my mind. I'd never felt so worthless in all my life. Pokeberry had trusted me, and I had failed her. The enormity of it all tore my heart out. I was inconsolable as I drove home.

We arrived home at four in the morning. I fed Hunky a bottle of milk and left him in the trailer for the night where I knew he'd be safe. I pulled a lounge chair and a blanket in there so I could stay with him. I set my alarm clock for three hours later...then, I crashed.

At eight o'clock, I unloaded Hunky and he followed me into the stall, his head turning in all directions as he cried for his mother. I cried with him and hugged him as tight as I could. But he didn't want me—he wanted his mother. I fed him another bottle of milk, wondering what I would do now.

As I closed the stall door, I looked around for Rose, but she was not to be seen. I wearily walked a short distance into the wooded area of the pasture before I saw her.

Wait—what's that beside her?

A small gray, woolly head standing beside Rose looked up at me.

I fell down on the ground and cried harder than I've ever cried before. All the pain that I had caused came to the forefront. Rose had delivered her baby jenny while her best buddy, Pokeberry, was being euthanized.

What a wonderful tribute to her friend!

After I'd cried it all out, I was finally able to smile through my tears. A new life had begun, not to take the place of the one that had been lost, but as a gentle reminder that life goes on, even through our trials and sorrows.

I named the new baby Dory to go with Hunky. Somehow, I knew everything would be Hunky Dory!

I bottle-fed Hunky every three hours until he was three months old, setting my alarm clock for each feeding just as though he was a human baby. I trekked from my house through the woods to the pasture through the rain, mud, cold, and darkness without fail to make sure Hunky was fed, and to this day, he still thinks I'm his mother. He's grown into a fine young jack, and he and Dory are as close as Pokeberry and Rose were.

There are too many unwanted animals in this country, so in Pokeberry's honor, I set up our farm as an animal rescue and sanctuary. Presently, the farm, named Sudie Belle Animal Sanctuary, is home to six horses and nine donkeys, most of them rescues from abusive situations, not to mention an assortment of dogs, cats, goats, chickens, ducks, geese, and a pot-bellied pig. Pokeberry's death opened my eyes to the fact that breeding animals is not necessary. All you have to do is look around and you'll find one that desperately needs a forever home.

The animal kingdom is overrun with unwanted animals, and it all stems from over-breeding and irresponsible owners like I was at that time. Even though we don't slaughter them in the United States, thousands of unwanted, perfectly good horses, donkeys, and mules are sold to disgusting kill buyers at auctions, and they ship them on over-crowded trailers to slaughter houses in Mexico and Canada. The last thirty-six hours of their precious lives are filled with unimaginable horror and agony as they are led to their deaths.

Pokeberry planted a seed of hope in my heart. In her honor, I've become an outspoken proponent for spaying, neutering, and gelding programs. She will never be forgotten. She taught me a lesson in humility and love. She loved me enough to entrust me with the care of her newborn son, and I didn't let her down. But as far as breeding animals goes, I learned a hard lesson. Never again! There's always an unwanted one out there who needs love, food, shelter, and a place to call home—a safe haven for weary little souls who depend on us to speak up for them.

About the Author—Carol Huff

Carol Huff lives a hectic life as owner (and Chief Poop-Scooper) of Sudie Belle Animal Sanctuary in Hartwell, Georgia. She finds inspiration for her writing amongst the forty-plus rescued animals who call her farm home. She is a regular contributor to *Chicken Soup for the Soul*, and her stories have also been published in *Country Magazine, Guideposts, Readers Digest, Country Extra Magazine, The Brayer, Ploughshares*, and *Simply Southern Magazine*. Aside from writing, her hobbies include horseback riding, interior decorating, and sleeping.

Kat's Story

Gil McDonald

We called her Kat. Even though she was a dog. I've always had this "thing" for calling my animals odd names, you see. I once had two canaries named Sausage and Chips, and when I was a youngster, I had two cats named Bootbrush and Polish. It was hardly surprising that a dog should be called Kat, was it?

Actually, that was only part of her name. She was a beautiful Scottish Border Collie and I thought we should give her a good Scottish name, so when she came to us at a cute and very fluffy eight weeks old, looking just like a miniature panda, I called her Katriona. She only ever got her Sunday name if she'd been naughty—and you know what puppies are like! In her first few months, she was often naughty; in fact, sometimes she was a downright catastrophe!

Guess what she got called then? Our surname was Constable; our naughty dog was "Katriona Catastrophe Constable"! It stuck for the rest of her life, not that she was naughty very often once she'd grown out of the puppy stage—just the opposite, in fact. She was so good and so easily trained that to this day, I have never known a more obedient or more intelligent dog. To tease her, we would sometimes give her the full "naughty name" and she would smile at us, showing all her teeth, as if she knew very well it was just a joke.

When Kat was around six months old, she somehow developed parvovirus—something like canine distemper. It's a killer, especially of young dogs, and we were afraid we were going to lose her. We fought hard to keep her alive and she fought even harder. By that time, she was fully housetrained, and even though she was almost dying, she wouldn't "do" anything in the house. She would drag herself to the door and wait for one of us to take her out. We had to hold her upright so that she could finish her business, then we'd carry her back indoors and wrap her up again in thick, fleecy blankets with hot water bottles.

Thankfully, she eventually pulled through, but the disease stunted her growth so she never grew to be quite as big as other bitches of the breed. It didn't stop her from being a little whirlwind, though! That dog had more energy than a dozen others put together. And everything she did, she did with a long, pink, wet tongue hanging out. Sometimes, it looked almost as if she was tasting the air, not just smelling it, as she went along with her tongue going in and out.

She only needed to be told something once and she would remember it forever. One day my mother visited, and Kat was so excited to see her, she started spinning round and holding on to the end of her tail. Mum laughed and said, "Take yourself for a walk." From then on, any time anyone said that to her, Kat would grab her tail and spin round and round.

Mum had been a top dog breeder for most of her adult life and had showed dogs for many years, even getting to the top worldwide championship show, Crufts, with her Samoyeds. She told us she had *never* come across any other dog who was as intelligent as Kat, and was certain that Kat wasn't *just* a dog, but a human in disguise, as she seemed to be able to understand everything we said with her huge vocabulary. We even had to resort to spelling certain words in order to try and fox her, but she soon learned how to spell those words, too!

My husband, Chris, was very keen on "do-it-yourself" projects. He had a large shed at the end of our long garden. Kat used to wander between me, in the house, and Chris, in his shed. If he wanted a brew, he'd write "put the kettle on" on a piece of paper and give it to Kat, saying, "Take it to your mum." Without fail, the message was delivered.

When it was time for a brew, or a meal, I would send her to get her dad. She would go down to the shed, get hold of his hand, and start to pull him toward the house, so he knew he was wanted. If he needed one of his tools, which was still in the house, he'd send a message for it. I would give it to Kat, who would carry the tool down to the shed. She even carried tools up ladders for him, sometimes. If I should happen to drop anything, she would dive straight in there and pick it up for me without being asked. I had only to point at something and say, "Get that," and she would go and bring the item to me.

I used to regularly walk her for a couple of miles across the fields to my parents' house and give her obedience training while we were out. She understood hand signals, and even *head* signals! I could shake my head for *no* and she would sit, or stop what she was doing. If I nodded, she would run ahead, or run back to me.

Just for fun, she would even climb trees. There was one on our route which had grown with a crooked bole, and it stuck out at a sharp angle about four feet off the ground. Kat would jump right up onto the branch and sit there, proudly wagging her tail and smiling like a "Cheshire Kat"!

The only things our lovely Kat was afraid of were cows and sheep! She was a Border Collie—a herding animal. They're *supposed* to be able to drive a flock of sheep anywhere. They are even supposed to get a herd of cows to go where they want them to. Not our Kat. Whenever we walked over the fields, if there were cows or sheep around, she would stick close to me and even make sure she was on the opposite side of me to the other animals. The cows were the worst. More inquisitive than sheep, they would often follow us down the fields, trying to get a closer look at Kat.

Of course, if there was livestock in the fields, I kept her on a lead. But her contortions were quite a sight as she tried to get away from the cows—and tied my legs up in knots with her lead! Strangely, she never seemed to worry about the horses who were sometimes in the fields. She was also very good at rounding up fluffy yellow chicks, which we told her were "babies." She would never hurt them, and could often be seen lying down with a collection of chicks using her as a jungle gym!

One year, we all went up to the Scottish Highlands for a camping holiday, taking our lovely Kat with us. It was a long journey, and we stopped halfway there for a break. I was walking Kat around, allowing her to stretch her legs, when a man approached us. Kat went into guard mode and placed herself in front of me, hair on end, growling at the man. He told me he was a professional shepherd and worked four Border Collies who'd won various competitions and cups over the years. He said he'd been watching us and asked if Kat was a working dog. When I told him she was just a family pet, he congratulated me, saying he'd never seen such a fit-looking and obedient Border Collie who was just a pet. High praise from a professional.

By this time, Chris and our little daughter, Sara, had joined us. I told Kat the man was a friend, so she had relaxed around him. She even obeyed him when he asked her to do a variety of things. He was thrilled with her and made a big fuss over her, which she loved. Then, he said he wanted to buy her from us. He offered us a huge amount of money. It would have helped us out tremendously—money was really tight at that time. But he could have offered us millions and we would never have parted with our Kat.

Kat loved us all, but she especially doted on Sara. She followed her around all over the place when she came back from school. Sara had been about eight when we got Kat, so they almost grew up together. Kat looked after Sara as if she were her real mum. Kat used to know exactly when Sara was due home from school, and was waiting by the door as soon as her friend walked in. Whenever Sara was ill, Kat would go and lie beside her until she felt better. If she was upset, Kat would snuggle up to her and lick her until she cheered up. That little dog would have done anything for her best friend.

All too soon though, her best friend grew up and got married. They couldn't have a dog in their rented house, so Kat stayed with us. She was upset, at first, and kept looking for Sara—but eventually, we all settled down to our new lives and Sara still got an ecstatic welcome whenever she came home.

Eventually, Kat began to slow down and started to show signs that something wasn't right. The vet said it was just that she was an old lady and we had to expect it—she was fourteen by then. Later that year, we took Kat to visit Sara and her husband. They had recently moved down to the other end of the country. It was a long drive, and Kat was quiet. When we got there, she greeted Sara with her usual exuberance and appeared quite happy for the few days we were there.

As we were leaving, Sara and Kat had a little snuggle through the open window of the car, and Sara didn't seem to want to let her go. During the drive back, Kat seemed quite unsettled. It was only after we got home that I realised she was bleeding. I thought it was her season, but it got very much worse over a couple of days, so I called the vet out. It was pyometra. There was nothing that could be done for her.

That afternoon, with the help of the vet, our beloved Kat went gently to sleep, held tightly in my arms in our kitchen. The hardest thing I ever had to do was to ring Sara and tell her that her best friend was gone.

After Kat left us, we were without animals of any kind for about four years, but now, I have two lovely Schnauzer "girls" to keep me company. I didn't want another Border Collie—I was afraid of comparing it to her, and that wouldn't have been fair.

Kat's going left a huge Collie-shaped hole in my heart, which—to this day—still fills with tears when I think about her.

Bless you, Katriona Catastrophe Constable.

About the Author—Gil McDonald

Gil McDonald, M.A., is proud to be the only English author signed to Prairie Rose Publications with her western romances. She is also published in the U.K., through Robert Hale of London, for whom she writes traditional, shoot-em-up westerns.

She is membership secretary for Lancashire Authors Association, which has worldwide membership.

Her life has been spent surrounded by animals, as her mother kept pet shops and grooming parlours, and was a show dog breeder and judge. Gil eventually ran her own animal rescue centre, which provided her with many stories.

Contact her through her website:
www.womanwholeads.webs.com

To Pauline with thanks.

G. McDonald

89

Best Buds

Meg Mims

I spoil dogs. The last thing I ought to do is rescue a needy dog. But our white, adorable-looking, but pain-in-the-butt Maltese Poodle—named Dusty since he looks like a dust-mop—was lonely. As a territorial fanatic, despite his tiny eight-pound body, he was a great watch dog.

Until he retired, the six-foot-tall mailman feared Dusty's wrath when he stepped on the porch. I had to restrain Dusty with a leash, harness, and even a muzzle whenever certain friends visited. The only things oblivious to Dusty? The squirrels in the back yard. Our previous poodle's "reign of terror" was over, and Dusty had no interest in the squirrels. They ruled, while Dusty drooled.

Unfortunately, when a friend dropped by one day, Dusty slipped out of my hands and made a lunge for the crotch. Luckily, the visitor wasn't hurt, just shocked. I had to do something—and finally agreed to consider getting a second dog. Maybe that would calm Dusty down. Maybe a new dog would become the pack alpha. Maybe a younger dog—quieter—would teach him a thing or two.

So one day, when I got a call about rescuing a dog, I thought hard. For a minute. "Bring him over," I said. "We'll see if Dusty and Benji get along."

My nephew soon arrived with the saddest looking dog —a Lhasa Apso mix, hairy, plump, and healthy-looking. His soulful eyes melted my heart. Benji sniffed my hand, curious, sniffed Dusty's butt and tolerated the return favor—but seemed more interested in the back yard. Especially the squirrels.

I asked a few questions, curious as to why any family would give up such a seemingly sweet dog. At only six, he had plenty of dog years left to his life. And he looked like he'd be a dog's dog.

According to my nephew, Benji had bitten a family's toddler grandchild. They didn't want to give him up, but had no choice. If I didn't take him, Benji was destined for the pound. I knew no one would take him due to his crime. He'd soon end up on death row, but he had such an interest in life. How could I reject Benji?

Most people visiting shelters have kids, and wanted dogs who tolerated kids. Benji had often been confined to a back room whenever the family's grandchildren visited. He'd also gotten into a bad habit of tearing up papers and creating messes out of boredom. Who could blame the family, wanting peace? And they also didn't want their grandchildren to become afraid of being bitten by a dog. I understood the dilemma.

Since our daughter was grown and gone, and we knew no little kids would be visiting our house, we talked it over. My husband and I agreed to give poor Benji a chance to live out the rest of his years as a member of our pack.

The worst part was watching my nephew leave and seeing Benji jump and bark at the backyard gate. He seemed to know he was being abandoned. I felt horrible. And Dusty clung to me like a leech. My eight-pound dog, overwhelmed by a dog three times his size, reacted to Benji's fear and tension. Benji finally gave up and returned to explore the yard, but I did worry a little. Would Dusty and Benji really get along? Or would there be trouble ahead? I had to half-drag the new dog into the house. *Oof.* Benji was hefty. I had to wonder what would happen come bedtime.

Remember, I spoiled my little lapdog Malti-Poo. Who could resist that cute little face, those large black eyes, his happy little yips? He didn't take up much room on our bed, between my husband and me, and we'd always allowed our Poodle on our bed, too.

Benji had settled down by evening, although he refused to eat. He kept watch out the window, as if expecting my nephew to return him to his "family." Poor thing. I had to wonder if Benji preferred staying in the kitchen. So we made a blanket bed for him, shut the sliding door, and turned out the lights.

Once we settled down, the howling soon started. Despite my husband's caution to give him time to adjust, I caved. I'm such a wimp. I really disliked the idea of keeping Benji apart from our "pack." I fetched him to our bedroom. Once again, I had to heft his bulk onto the mattress. He settled down at once on the bed's end.

One thing I discovered—Benji was a great foot warmer. Within a few days, Dusty inched closer to him, as well, instead of being a "dog bolster" between us. *Hallelujah.*

I really hoped Benji would clean up well since I could barely see his eyes, much less his body shape. Off to the groomers he went, and gave them no trouble at all. After being shaved down, Benji looked like a new dog—trim, handsome, his coat smoother and far more beige than a mixed shade of dark brown and tan. I totally fell in love. And Benji absolutely loved riding in the car. I even drove around with him while he watched the scenery out the window, happy and interested.

Perhaps Benji hoped he'd find his way back to his family. Instead, we returned to our house. He didn't seem to mind, though, and soon took over "squirrel patrol" with relish in the back yard. We also established a daily routine for both dogs.

Every morning, I sang the "breakfast song": "It's breakfast time, it's breakfast time, it's breakfast time, it's breakfast time!" I placed their food bowls at opposite ends of the kitchen. Previously, Dusty would "graze"; now, he quickly learned that if he didn't eat it all, Benji would polish it off. I also sang a "suppertime" song: "Suppertime, suppertime, sup-sup-suppertime…" Again, they both ate every bite. Whew. No more grazing. When we ate, Dusty had always been a beggar; Benji taught him to wait without barking or jumping in case any morsels were coming. Another victory.

Every day, or depending on the weather, I harnessed both dogs and walked them together. Benji proved to be a good walker; Dusty ran back and forth, lunged, barked at other dogs, but I learned that I couldn't keep them on separate leashes. I'd end up with one dog ahead and the other one winding around my legs. I bought a "Y" attachment, which kept both dogs side by side; Benji taught Dusty to walk nice. Another victory!

Benji also came to love our cushy green plaid sofa, blocking the very large front window. Dusty always jumped up to the seat cushion, and then easily up on top; Benji wanted to, as well, but had more trouble. I ended up boosting him onto the seat, and then he learned to scramble up the back cushion to lie next to Dusty. They could both watch out the window—and unfortunately, Benji acquired Dusty's habit of "mail call alarm" within a week. Oh, well. Still, we loved seeing both dogs lying on top, napping in the sun, or sprawled on opposite ends on the seat cushions.

Seeing them become "best buds" certainly made our decision the right one. If only it could have lasted.

Autumn arrived. Both dogs really disliked getting their paws wet in rain or snow-packed in winter, although Benji would chase squirrels through the drifts—and nearly caught them, at times. We dressed up both dogs for Christmas with little Santa hats, and I made a "best buds" ornament for the tree. Benji enjoyed digging into his new stocking for treats. He was far more content than when he first arrived, lying at my feet, although he didn't mind his daily "smoochies"—he'd stretch up with his paws and I'd rub his head and ears. He also tolerated bedtime "kisses." Barely.

Winter ended, springtime brought flowers and longer walks, and spring turned into early summer. Benji and Dusty loved sitting together by the front full-glass door, watching the cars and kids pass by to school or play.

Dusty was more of a "house" dog—he went out to do his business, and returned. Benji, however, enjoyed exploring inside the garage and behind it. He'd disappear for fifteen or twenty minutes, and sometimes longer. I often had to whistle for him and track him down—and there he'd be, behind the garage, nosing through the weeds.

He may have met his match there.

I first noticed him scratching his side a lot. Usually dogs do scratch, and Benji was more of a "dog's dog," so I didn't think much of it at the time. Until I noticed at bedtime his side had a large discolored spot. It looked swollen. I put ointment on it, thinking the skin was inflamed from his scratching. The next day, I called the vet. By the time I could get an appointment the following day, the spot had grown much larger; the discoloration looked worse. And the vet had no idea what to make of it.

Benji grew very sick, wouldn't eat, and was clearly suffering. Long story short, by the time we realized the infection had gotten into his blood, we did everything we could: putting him on multiple medications, tests up the wazoo, and treatments so strong, he might not survive that. The vet believed it may have been an insect bite, but we had no real proof. Benji died in my arms, knowing he was loved.

I still grieve for that sweet rescue dog. I wrote *Santa Paws*, a holiday romance novella featuring a rescue dog inspired by Benji, except a little friskier in causing trouble; I found a photo for the cover that resembled his soulful eyes. And I gave him a loving home with a loving family, despite reality's less-happy ending.

We still have Dusty, and he's growing old without his best bud Benji. One day soon, we're bound to say goodbye to him. All dogs go to heaven—their own version of long naps, delicious treats, belly rubs, ear scratches, and lots of sloppy kisses.

If only all our best bud dogs could live forever.

About the Author—Meg Mims

Award-winning author Meg Mims writes western historical mystery and romance, sweet Christmas-themed romance novellas that include rescue dogs and cats, tackles her to-be-read pile between deadlines, and enjoys tearooms, flowers, and gardening. She also is one-half of the D.E. Ireland writing team for the Edwardian-era Eliza Doolittle and Henry Higgins historical mysteries. Meg will debut her teddy bear cozy mystery series next year for Kensington Books, writing as Meg Macy. Website: www.megmims.com

How to Hatch a Baby Duck

Tina Holt

The second year that we had ducks on our farmette, when I was seven, one of the lady quackers laid eggs. She wasn't a particularly good or experienced mother, for she left the eggs scattered around the duck coop, not in a nest. She was more like the Easter Bunny than Mother Goose.

My mother suspected that the eggs were fertile, and it broke her heart to see them abandoned in the mud and weather. After a long bout of thinking, she collected six of the recently laid eggs and brought them inside to incubate herself, which was an activity she didn't know how to do.

At first, I thought she meant that she was going to sit on them. I saw the obvious problems with that and told her so. "You're too big! You'll squish them!" and, more importantly, "If you're sitting on the eggs, who will make dinner and fold the laundry?" Followed by a timid, "Can I have a turn, too?"

My brothers were more supportive of her efforts. "Don't worry, Mom, we'll build you a nice nest, like the one Big Bird has." They were serious about this project, and went so far as to make a list of items they'd need. Sticks and twigs. Twine. Mud to seal up the gaps.

Mom went along with the game for a little while, before assuring me—and disappointing the boys—that she didn't mean she'd *hatch* the eggs like a mother duck. She meant to *incubate* them—like in a laboratory. With mention of the word "laboratory," she recaptured our interest. Just the word sparked images of important-looking white lab coats, bubbling potions, and lightning.

In the 1970's, Queen Anne's County, Maryland, was mostly farmland. Mom and Dad had moved there from Baltimore to raise their kids in what they considered an idyllic childhood setting. Being from the Big City, there was a learning curve to living in the country. One of the resources my parents discovered was the county's farm extension agent. Someone was almost always on hand to answer questions as simple as "How does one plant grass seed?" to more complicated ones such as "How do I hatch baby ducks?" It was this magic number that Mom prepared to contact now.

She was anxious about talking on the phone, and rarely made calls. When she did, we knew it had to be a Serious and Important Matter. I don't know how long it took her to muster the courage to pick up the phone. She sat at the dining room table with the shoebox of eggs in front of her, pen and paper at the ready, and a pack of cigarettes within arm's reach.

"Hello? Yes. This is Mrs. Hagan. I'm calling about my ducks."

The call didn't last too long, and Mom mostly nodded and said, "Mm-hm," and "Oh, I see." When she hung up the phone, it was hard to read her face.

My brothers and I looked at her anxiously. She lit a cigarette and sighed.

"He said it wouldn't work."

Our faces fell. We loved the idea of raising baby ducks.

"I told him I understood that, but to tell me how one would go about hatching eggs." She took a puff. "He said we could rent an incubator from the office."

Our faces fell farther. We barely had money for gas. There was no way we could afford to rent an incubator for eggs that were probably rotten.

"I told him I didn't want to do that, and to tell me how to make one, anyway."

She pushed the butt into the ashtray. "He laughed and told me there was a way, but that it wouldn't work."

She smiled. "So, let's make an incubator."

The homemade incubator that the extension agent described was a medium-sized cardboard box with a 100-watt lightbulb. Mom set the box on a TV tray in the corner of the dining room, near a wall socket. She took the lampshade off of a nursery lamp and suspended it upside down into the box, where it was held up by two pieces of spare paneling.

We marked each egg with an "X" on one side before placing them into the box. We would need to turn the eggs at least three times every day, just like a mother duck would do, to make sure the whole egg got maximum warmth. The X would help us keep track of the turns.

We also put a bowl of water in the box to add moisture to the air, since the continuous heat of the lightbulb would make the inside of the box as dry as a desert. The bowl was a favorite of mine—a melamine cereal bowl with a jumping clown at the bottom with the words "All Gone!" I didn't mind sharing—not if it meant ducklings.

Days turned into weeks, and the box turned from an interesting curiosity to an invisible piece of furniture. We didn't have lab coats, and scribbling on the clipboard and looking at the eggs with a magnifying glass got boring after just a couple of days.

The eggs sat in the box, day in and day out, seemingly doing nothing. My thoughts drifted away from fuzzy baby ducks to kite flying and softball tryouts. The backyard was still springtime muddy, but the sunshine was warm and lovely. The grownup, outdoor ducks carried on as usual, rooting in the mud for bugs and paddling in the ditch. They hadn't even noticed that the eggs were gone.

The king of the yard was a mean and fat rooster. He disliked people, and his squawking and flapping terrified anyone, person or animal, who came within twenty feet of him.

One night, we had a terrible storm that brought down the metal tool shed. We found out the next day that the rooster was trapped underneath the rubble. He survived the accident, but not without injury. His head was split open from a piece of metal siding. From that moment on, he was the sweetest creature on earth. The shed lobotomy made him docile and cuddly, though his constant crowing at all hours of the day drove everyone in the family slightly mad. He adopted the silly ducks, following them around and earnestly trying to communicate his secret knowledge.

A month into the experiment, around day twenty-eight, was my day to turn the eggs. I noticed a crack in one. It looked like a squiggly K, and it hadn't been there that morning. I was afraid I had done something wrong; perhaps I had turned the egg too swiftly, or squeezed the shell too tightly. I called Mom over, prepared for the worst. She peeked in over my shoulder, kissed the top of my head and told me to get my brothers—it was time.

We crowded around to watch. It took a long time, and we had to take turns peering through the crack of the paneling at the top of the box, but it happened. The egg trembled, and the crack widened. Black matted down pressed through a tiny opening. We were too excited to speak. The opening grew, exposing more down. Slowly, the shell broke away, revealing wrinkled gray legs and a gray beak with a tiny pearl of an egg tooth. We had a baby duck!

At first, it didn't look cute and fluffy, confusing all expectations I had of ducklings. This creature was moist and floppy, and the way it lay panting on the bottom of the box made me wonder if it would survive. By bedtime, though, the duckling was dry, sitting upright with its legs tucked underneath it and peeping softly. I was immensely proud.

When I woke in the morning, we had three ducklings. There was much debate over the naming of these enchanted beings before we settled on the best: Quackers, Waddles, and...Craig.

A few hours later, with all of us gathered around, Mom sat down at the table, pen and paper at the ready, a pack of cigarettes within reach. She picked up the phone.

"Hello? Yes. This is Mrs. Hagan. I called last month about incubating duck eggs?" Her face broke into a wide grin. "I'm calling today to ask what to feed them."

About the Author—Tina Holt

I'm a nature-loving cheese enthusiast with a particular fondness for invertebrates. My greatest wish is to see an octopus in the wild. I live with my husband and three daughters in a 111-year-old Dutch Colonial that's probably not haunted. I've written for previous editions of *Memories from Maple Street, Highlights Magazine for Children, Knowonder!, Sea Urchins Magazine, and* Bedtime-story.com.

Horse Tales

Tanya Hanson

When they whicker, the horses laugh, sing, tell me stories only I can hear. And I love it all.

Of course, I expected the local horse rescue to rescue me. To ease the hurt after losing the third of our three Labradors. I needed some animal sugar bad, but travel and out-of-town grandkids made a new pet all but impossible for a while. However, I refused to volunteer at the county animal shelter. As I warned my husband, I'd bring all the dogs and cats home.

"Then you should volunteer here." He pointed to the

California Coastal Horse Rescue's booth at the county fair one hot August day six years ago. "You can't bring a horse home."

No, I couldn't. I'm a California beach girl living on the Central Coast on a trim, tidy cul-de-sac with tiny yards. No corrals. No barns. I hadn't sat a horse since Girl Scout Camp. I knew nothing about them.

"Then learn," my husband further declared. "After all, you write western romances. It'll be great research."

I did. I learned. And I fell in love. Each of the horses there has touched my heart. Each has a story. And although they have sad beginnings, they all get happy endings. The rescue's goal is rehabilitation and adoption. We hope each horse will find a forever home, but if they don't, they stay in our wonderful valley until the time comes to cross the Rainbow Bridge.

We volunteers both weep and rejoice when one of "the kids" gets adopted.

We cry and hold each other—and the horse—when the time comes for one of our sweethearts to "run free."

Such as Lover Girl. This beautiful Thoroughbred was found running loose a few years ago in the tony hills of Malibu. Well, horses are expensive to feed and tend. During hard times, yes, they're often abandoned. This pretty girl managed to find any nearby stable and flirt with the boys. She found her way to our rescue and was lovingly adopted by Geraldine. Now, Geraldine, like me, is a beach girl—so Lover Girl was privately boarded at the rescue. Good for us all. We got to love her, then. And get to love her memory, still.

Last Thanksgiving break, I brought my nine-year-old grandson to the rescue for the first time. Lover Girl leaned her head toward him, and he asked if he could pet her. He did, with wonder and awe. "Gramma, she's the first horse I ever touched."

I have a picture of that magical moment. Two days after Christmas, Lover Girl died suddenly from a stomach ailment she'd brought along with her. My grandbaby and I cried together.

I still get tears just thinking about their first touch.

In whispers, the other volunteers and I admit we almost like animals better than most people. There's something about animals in need that make me realize I don't really have any problems at all. If I think I do, well, I come to the Rescue. Just being there makes me feel better.

And inspired. Of late, I've set two fictional stories at a rescue just like ours. In a middle-grade story, you'll meet a gentle, intelligent Warmblood-Paint cross nicknamed Fang. Wait a minute. You'll learn why.

The rescue sits on ten donated acres in a small valley in West Ventura County, California, about twelve miles inland from the Pacific Ocean. The ten-mile-by-three-mile valley stretches east-west across the foothills of the Topa Topa Mountains between Santa Barbara and Los Angeles. In the late winter, the scent of orange blossoms drifts across the rescue because our little ranchette was once an orange grove. Quite a few trees remain to give shade and delicious fruit. And because of our geography—most valleys go north-south—we experience a phenomenon during many sunsets.

The Pink Moment.

The mountains and valley are thickly forested with California live oak trees. While sunset usually turns the western sky over the ocean rosy and spectacular, this area is one of the few in the world where sunset comes from the east and glows across the mountains.

Like a mirror, the Topa Topas reflect the sun from the west and start to blush. The sunlight diffuses across the mountains in gorgeous shades of pink for a few breathless minutes. Somehow, you can feel the quiet.

The "pink moment" doesn't happen with every sunset, but I've been lucky enough to be feeding the horses their dinner at just the right time.

And I'm lucky enough to know Cheyenne, aka "Fang." Oh, my career as a school teacher taught me well—you don't pick favorites. No teacher's pets. No special treatment.

But Cheyenne... His story, like most of them, breaks my heart and would wound my soul forever if it weren't for all the love surrounding our little rescue. After horrific abuse and torture with cattle prods, this beautiful Warmblood-Paint cross came to the Rescue anxious, broken, and unable to trust any human at all.

He'd surge to the farthest corner of his stall whenever anybody approached, eyes wide and white with nerves—if not downright terror. Slowly, he began to feel the love. His special sponsor is Andrea, the president of our little piece of heaven. Slowly, surely, he learned to trust again. Andrea nicknamed him "Fang" because "Shy Anne" sounded too girly.

I remember my tears the day Cheyenne, er...Fang, finally allowed Andrea to saddle and mount him in our big training ring. After many patient months, he'd learned to love and trust again. Oh, tears and smiles both the day I chaperoned a high school service day— Cheyenne came to a teenage boy and rested his muzzle on the kid's shoulder.

Indeed, Cheyenne has gotten to know me. Oh, we're

not a riding stable. I won't be riding him. Highly skilled volunteers with much experience do the exercising after significant training and time. However, I do my part. I rock at feeding the horses—and yes, mucking. For what goes in must come out.

When I tell friends what a great mucker I've become, they wrinkle their noses and say, "Ick." But it's good exercise and not an unpleasant odor—and above all, it's a great way to get to know the horses. I spend Tuesday afternoons making sure our horses—fifteen at present—get their supper on time and go to sleep in clean stalls.

Therefore, the horses whicker whenever I approach with their chuckles, their songs. No matter which day of the week, or the time of day. They see me: *food.*

Yet, it does go deeper than that. I know they love me. Cheyenne, well, I get kisses from him—but more than that, I can see the tales in his eyes, the stories he wants to tell. I don't always know the journey, but I know he'll get his happy ending. And along the way, I realize how much he helps me find my own way. I see my reflection in those deep brown eyes ringed with white, and know he sees me back.

Thing is, life isn't all a smooth ride for humans, either. Complications, sadness, problems often rear their ugly heads. And writing is a solitary occupation. But the rescue has taught me where I need to go when I can't find answers on my own.

I talk to the horses. One in particular, because Cheyenne answers me back.

Last fall, I had a professional problem and was sorely tempted to blast off a hasty, nasty email. I know, I know. Nothing in cyberspace ever dies, so I did hold my fingers still on the *send* button. But the pain and confusion slammed hard, and it happened to be a Tuesday. My feeding day.

My day of answers and joy.

I came to the Rescue and talked to Cheyenne. As always, he pushed his handsome face against mine for a quick kiss. "What should I do?" I asked into his deep brown stare. "Do I send the email? I'm in the right, you know. It's hard to take when somebody else is wrong...and rude."

He listened carefully, calmly. Then, he took a deliberate step back. His gaze never left mine.

I trusted his answer. I did the same. Figuratively. I took a step back from the situation for a few days. And guess what? The problem got solved with no hasty, nasty words.

The next Saturday, I came to the Rescue to teach my monthly little class for new volunteers. First thing I did was tell Cheyenne he'd been right. I'd listened to his advice. I'd held off.

I'd stepped back.

He looked me straight on and...yup...nodded his head five or six times.

Through the love of a horse, I'd found my truth.

But life never leaves me alone. It's full of hills and valleys, peace and pain, hither and yon. Yes and no, and not to mention *maybe*.

Easter time this year came after five weeks of explosive decisions concerning the welfare of an elderly family member. Frankly, my husband and I were exhausted, with stress past the boiling point.

At least, the grandkids laughed and dyed eggs and hunted for their treasures a hundred times on a beautiful Easter Day.

Then, reality smacked again. Fortunately, Tuesday came around, and the hectic schedule had finally freed me enough to come feed. The "family gunk", as I called it, had kept me away from the rescue for a few weeks, and I needed the horses more than ever. Once again, I talked to my Cheyenne. He listened. He looked into my eyes.

Then, very slowly, he closed his lids tight for five or six seconds. It wasn't a windy day. No dust. No flies. When he opened his eyes again, I checked. Nothing going on.

His eyes drifted closed again. And I got it. He wanted me to sleep on the decision-making. No rush. No hurries. Take my time. No regrets.

And as you can predict, I slept on it. And when I woke the next day, I found more truth.

In my life, I know I've helped rescue these horses—but so often, they've rescued me right back.

About the Author—Tanya Hanson

Western romance author Tanya Hanson is ever on the trail of a tender tale, and the horses at her local rescue always take her there. Helping feed them and muck stalls keeps her from being chained to the computer. Any other spare time finds this California native traveling with her firefighter husband, or hanging out at the beach with the grandkids. Please find her at
www.tanyahanson.com and
www.petticoatsandpistols.com

Embry and Jessica a few days after his hospital stay in Stillwater, OK.

Two Hundred Pounds of Love

Cheryl Pierson

I always wanted a dog. But growing up in my family was unsettled. Dad had a job that meant lots of unscheduled call outs at all hours. He worked in the Oklahoma oilfields as a chemical engineer—and when they needed his expertise, he had to go. Sometimes, he'd leave in the middle of the night, if they called, and we might not see him for three or four days.

We lived in Seminole, Oklahoma, at the time. Both my parents were from a very small town in the southeastern part of the state, about a hundred miles from Seminole.

With Mom and Dad both being the eldest in their families, we spent many weekends traveling back and forth. My two sisters had both gone away to college by the time I turned eight—so there would have been no one to care for a puppy. It would have been an inconvenience.

During those days—the '60's and '70's—boarding animals wasn't done like it is presently. And in our small-town neighborhood, fencing yards was almost unheard of.

So...I had cats. And though I thoroughly loved each and every cat I ever had, I still secretly yearned for a puppy.

After one nag too many, my ever-practical father said, "Wouldn't you be sad if your dog got run over by a car?"

Of course, I said, "Yes."

"Well," he went on, "before you were born, when Annette and Karen were little, we had two puppies who got hit by cars. We didn't have a fenced yard then, and we don't have one here, either. A cat can get out of the street quicker than a dog. Let's just stick with Old Tom, shall we?"

Put like that, there wasn't much I could do but agree—and it sounded like even if I *could* have had a dog, there would certainly not be room for two pets in our home. I wasn't about to give up my white cat, Tom. He'd been my best buddy for a couple of years by then.

But everything changed seven years ago.

My own daughter, a young, single, twenty-something, bought a small house. The back yard was huge. The neighborhood wasn't the best. Jessica decided a dog would not only be good company, but also offer a bit of protection.

She and her brother, Casey, trekked down to one of the local shelters in search of her new puppy. As Fate would have it, there was a litter of beautiful Great Pyrenees-Anatolian Shepherd puppies that were looking for homes. *Nine* of them! Each one had been named for a character from the then-popular *Twilight* series.

Sweet little Embry was the one she chose—and he mutually chose her. A match made in heaven.

She and Casey brought Embry right over to our house to show him off. He was a bundle of solid snow-white fur, for he wasn't old enough to have gotten his gray and brindle markings yet.

A quick look at his paws told my husband and me he was going to be considerably larger than the seventy to eighty pounds the shelter workers had predicted.

Embry was the perfect companion for Jessica, but he was lonely, with her at work so much. She began to bring him to "Grandma and Grandpa's" house so he wouldn't have to be alone when she worked so many hours.

I was enthralled. I finally had a dog—and he was treated like a king.

But Embry had times when he was very, very sick. He would lose his balance, and walk around and around in circles. He'd lie on the floor, panting—and let me tell you, it scared us all to death. We'd load him up and get him to the vet, only to be told, "I'm not sure what it is...maybe someone threw some poison meat over the fence..."

He began to spend more time at our house—where, surrounded by dog lovers on all sides, we were certain no one would do anything to try to hurt him.

But it happened again, when he'd been back over at Jessica's, and so back to the vet we went.

"Maybe he ate some kind of plant that's poisonous,"

the vet guessed.

A landscaper was hired to dig up all the wild vegetation in Jessica's yard and haul it away, as well as the flower beds. Decades of lovely flower planting by previous owners was gone in one afternoon.

Though Embry recovered after a few days each time, we still didn't know why it happened. It was heart wrenching—and frightening—to go through.

The third time it happened was the worst. He wouldn't eat—not even a warm, buttery biscuit. And he would only lap water out of our palms, then turn away. He was miserable, and we were more afraid—if possible—than we'd ever been.

This time, another vet looked at him and was also mystified. She suggested we "put him down". *But why?* No one knew what was wrong, and he had recovered in the past.

She finally said she might be able to call the Oklahoma State University School of Veterinary Medicine and see if they would look at him. She made the call, and they agreed. We drove straight to Stillwater, clinging to our last hope.

Upon arriving, our spirits were lifted immediately. The young veterinary students looked at Embry as a challenge—and they had the desire to help. One of the vet professors walked into the room and, after watching a few minutes, said, "I think I may know what the problem is, but we need to do some testing. Why don't you all leave him with us for a couple of days and let us see what we can do?"

As Jessica and I left to drive home in the darkness, we were cautiously optimistic. At least, there was some hope for our sweet boy!

Jessica called several times to check on Embry over the next three days. He had been diagnosed with "steroid responsive meningitis"—a disease that's not common, but one that the vet instructor had seen two cases of already that year. Thankfully, because he was aware of the disease and though the cause was unknown, he had successfully treated the earlier cases. We were happy to know Embry was in capable hands, and that the professor knew what to do.

Embry had to be given massive doses of steroids, and as soon as those began to work, he started to become his old self again. The veterinary students bought canned tuna and canned chicken, and offered him delicacies such as pepperoni pizza to entice him to eat—and it worked!

They cared enough to try to find just the right thing to whet his appetite enough to eat, and get him "back on track" again. Once the steroids took effect, his dizziness gradually disappeared. He stopped feeling sick and began to eat and drink. The only thing that remained was getting him back home with us to be babied like never before.

On the fourth day, they let us know we could come pick him up. With joyful hearts, Jessica and I made the hour-and-a-half drive to Stillwater to get him. We couldn't believe the miraculous recovery he had made! Tail wagging, he hurried to us, licking our faces as we knelt down on the floor beside him. His brown eyes were bright and full of life again, and he almost looked as if he were smiling.

"Let's go home!" he seemed to say.

We were all too happy—even as we paid the bill—to see him looking so much better. The trip back to Oklahoma

City was much happier than when we'd driven that stretch of highway only four days earlier, unsure if there was any help to be had for Embry. He would have to take steroids for the rest of his life, but at least we knew we had something to control his sickness.

Time passed, and Jessica had to move to a place with no fence. Since Embry was already spending so much time with us, it was only natural that he would just move in with "Grandma and Grandpa."

We have been so happy to have him permanently. Great Pyrenees dogs are herders by the nature and instinct of their breed, and Embry has proved that time and again.

My husband Gary, daughter Jessica, son Casey, and I are his "herd"—and he is ferociously protective. When he has all his "cows" together, he is completely content. He has been known to decide it's "family time" and round us up. Even though Jessica and Casey are grown and don't live here anymore, Embry will come into my office and flip my hand off the keyboard with his nose. If I don't come immediately, he puts his paw on my chair, letting me know, "I really mean it. Come on!"

When I get up to follow him, he leads me right into the living room where my husband is, and stops to pick up his favorite stuffed animal. He holds it in his mouth until I sit down. Only then will he set the animal down the floor in front of my chair.

Content that Gary and I are both in the same room where we can be watched and guarded, Embry lies on the floor between our chairs, his paws on Gary's feet.

A job well done!

It's no secret that I tell people Embry is my "third child"—even *he* knows it.

If Gary tries to sneak off to another room for a snack of chips or popcorn, Embry comes to tell on him. He insists I follow him, and when we get to "the scene of the crime," he stands and stares accusingly until the snack is shared.

Embry has brought us so many laughs and so much joy, I can't imagine life without him. Two hundred pounds of love is ours, and his name is Embry!

About the Author—Cheryl Pierson

Cheryl is a native Oklahoman with eight novels to her credit as well as numerous short stories and novellas. Founding Prairie Rose Publications with Livia Reasoner is a dream-come-true for her—there's something new every day. Helping other authors is at the top of her list, and she enjoys every minute of it. She has two grown children and lives with her husband and her rescue dog, Embry, in Oklahoma City.

See Prairie Rose Publications' website for more of Cheryl's work: http://prairierosepublications.com

Facebook: https://www.facebook.com/cheryl.pierson.92

Touser the Born-Again Poodle

L.D.B. Taylor

Touser was a giveaway.

I've never known who cared for him during his first days, and I don't suppose I ever will.

But I do know who cared for him during his last. That teary, handful of days...*and doesn't it seem longer than that, thinking back?* Days spent cradling him, gently; whispering our goodbyes; trying our best to let him go.

****

Annie Rose spotted him first.

Tiny, black curly hair, a stub of a tail—Annie Rose pointed one chubby finger at the puppy hiding beneath grandma's wooden porch. "Aw...Sweet..." Baby teeth smiled up at me, her green eyes shining. "Mama—I take that puppy home?"

And before I could open my mouth to say, "No, that's Grandma's neighbor's new puppy." Thinking *good grief— the last thing we need is another dog. Just imagine what Scott'd say. Not to mention, that critter looks suspiciously like a poodle—which would immediately earn my husband's scorn.*

Yes, before I had a chance to voice an objection, Grandma—my mother—and her neighbor, Mae, gave one another identical smiles and eerily cooed in one voice, "Why, isn't that a *wonderful* idea?"

Managing to snag and hold onto a handful of curly black hair just before it disappeared entirely beneath the porch, Mae held the cowering, filthy puppy out for Annie Rose to pet.

"Obviously, it's meant for little Rexie, here, to live with you!" My mother laughed as Annie Rose leaned out and hugged Rexie, burying her face in his twig-snarled curls.

"Uh...I dunno—" I began, watching my three-year-old daughter cuddling the dog. Her four-year-old brother meandered down the porch steps toward us. His pace quickened, eyes lit up at the sight of a puppy. "I mean— we already have three dogs. And...well—" I lowered my voice. "Isn't he a poodle? I don't think Scott'll..."

"Oh, Scott will love this dog!" Mom said. "Won't he, Mae?"

"Of course he will." Mae, who'd never even set eyes on my husband, nodded. "And just look how these sweet children have taken to Rexie!" Jess had joined his sister, the two of them sitting on the grass, happily mauling the bedraggled, sleepy-looking puppy. Mae and my mother smiled wide at me. "I just don't see how you can go home without him!"

Evidently, neither did I.

****

A year or so later, Touser—we rechristened him during that first drive home—had grown into a four-pound horror of opinionated, ornery, yapping canine.

"That is the orneriest dog on the planet," Scott would mutter, slathering antibiotic ointment onto the angry scratches left by Touser during the hated bath time.

"Touser nipped at me again!" Jess would roar, sticking out his tongue at the screen door where Touser stood guard over his domain, and growling low on the other side.

"That flippin' dog ate another one of my sandals..." Being the only member of the family who actually put such things away, I never quite understood how this could have happened. Did Touser somehow manage to maneuver through the dog gates, open my closet door, and then, head tilted, stand considering—choosing the tastiest looking of my footwear from the closet shelf? Did he have an accomplice—a chimpanzee, presumably—we were unaware of?

Yet another mystery.

Yes, Touser was an obnoxious, undersized, canine monstrosity who hated trees, leaves, shrubbery, flowers, shoes, coming indoors, or going outdoors. Most especially, he hated baths or being groomed...and evidently, he hated people on principle.

Except for Annie Rose.

Our Girl Annie Rose was Touser's moon and stars. His shining light. The gravy upon his dog chow, the crunch of his doggy biscuit. Yes, even the cream of his Oreo— had he been allowed to eat Oreos.

She could dress Touser up in doll clothes, buttoned and zipped, right down to a ruffled bonnet, tiny socks, and cunning booties. He allowed her to brush his hair with her doll's comb and then wheel him around and around the back yard in her baby carriage, carefully swaddled in blankets. The tip of his glistening black nose was just visible. She could load him into the back seat of her plastic toy family van alongside a battered teddy bear and two half-naked Barbies—and all the while, the maniacal, nipping, meaner-than-a-hornet Touser would calmly and obediently *stay*.

And just why this was, we couldn't quite figure out. We watched in disbelief from the porch as Annie Rose scooped Touser from the baby carriage, sliding him into the stroller, and plopping a sunbonnet on his head. His wagging tail, his wriggling, twisting body obviously begged her for *one more pet* as they set off toward their tea party on the basketball court.

But somewhere in my mind—the same spot, I expect, which has always and will forever believe all dogs do indeed go to heaven—I believed Touser could see Our Girl's extra twenty-first chromosome shining through. Dogs, being in most ways superior to people despite their *chewing up my best shoes, peeing on the carpet, and lookit that disgustin' dog eating the turkey poop* ways— sense the true nature of people. They know deep-down-inside of a person's spirit; that light shining from a person's eyes as they smile, reaching out a soft, certain hand to stroke a dog's neck or scratch that spot *right there*, near their left ear which they can't quite get to.

And so it was for nearly eight years; we—Scott, our four boys, and I—tolerated ornery ole Touser. Tolerated his nips and growls; got through those days when he'd somehow escape our fenced yard—causing me to run hither and yon about the neighborhood, inevitably dressed in my horrible house clothes, peeking behind the neighbor's shrubbery, hollering for him like an idiot. And, once found, I was forced to carry him for blocks myself because the boys were afraid to touch him and Annie Rose was at home, mourning her lost dog, tearfully watching out the window for his return.

We tolerated Touser because he loved Our Girl, and she loved him.

And then, one day—and just when it was and how did it really happen, I'd love to know—well, one day, Touser found Jesus...

...and became a Born-Again Poodle.

You can laugh if you want to—most people have. Scott claimed Touser had either gone crazy or become senile. And to be honest, I'm the only one who really believed Touser had somehow gone and got himself religion—no doubt during one of his infamous "yard escapes."

But none of that makes what happened any less true.

One sudden, fine day, all the orneriness and spite simply departed Touser's body—leaving him a slightly larger, older version of his old sweet puppy self. There he was, waggling his tail at Annie Rose's brothers—who, not having been born yesterday, regarded him with some suspicion. He jumped at our legs with no teeth and growls—just asking for pets, this time. He did the happy-spinning-my-stubby-tail-till-it's-a-blur dance every time one of us arrived home.

And, strangest of all, Scott—formerly his most hated nemesis, Dreaded Giver of Baths, Maniacal Master of the Hair and Nail Clipper—became, next to Annie Rose, Touser's most beloved human on the planet.

So life changed just a bit at our house.

And then, as it tends to, life changed just a bit more.

****

Annie Rose was the first to spot it.

"Touser's getting a big butt," she said. She pointed at Touser who, it was true, seemed to have gained some weight in his rear quarters.

So Scott bundled Touser up onto his lap to take a better look, discovering what we immediately knew was some type of growth.

Inoperable, said the first vet we took him to. And the second. And, yes, the third.

All of them advised us to *"put him down"*. It was the kindest thing to do. The tumor would grow, his organs would begin to fail, his days would be spent in misery and pain.

But he wasn't in pain now. Not today. Today, Touser was a puppy hurtling across the yard alongside his boys, sharing a peanut butter sandwich with his best girl on the lawn, and curling up on his bed, dog-pile-snoozing with his canine buddies.

And why, I always wonder, why the words "put him down"? Put him down—set him aside, leave him be. Click off the light, shut the door—cast him from your mind.

So, we stepped into the hardest days of being a dog's person; days spent watching and waiting. Looking for changes in Touser's behavior. Was he eating all right?

122

Did he seem tired—sleeping more, sleeping less? Did he still greet his Annie Rose with happy jumps, follow Scott around the yard—tail, a delighted blur. Were his eyes clear, his energy up, his ear-splitting, obnoxious, yipping bark still echoing around the yard, sounding the alarm: *A suspicious oak leaf is floating along the grass!*

And, you know, he was.

For five years, we watched Touser. As his rear end became more and more ungainly, people begin to ask us, "What kind of dog is that, anyway?" Explaining his condition to our boys and Annie Rose was difficult. Annie Rose cried and shook her head "No!" Nothing could be wrong with Touser. He was just a puppy—*her* puppy.

For five years, we kept a careful eye on Touser—and how grateful I am we did. Those years were perhaps the happiest of Touser's life.

He had his girl to love him, his boys no longer afraid of growls and nips, and his second favorite person, Scott, to tag along with outside. And me—sneaking him treats, making certain his was the most comfy dog bed, and letting him snuggle on the couch while the other dogs laid at our feet.

Then came the morning when Touser didn't want to hop out of bed and run outside. Instead, he remained upon his cushion, gimlet eyes drooping, tail wagging slow as we petted and soothed him. His labored breathing told us his time had finally come.

But how sudden it was! One day he was running with the other dogs outside, black curls shining. And now—*this*; lying near the fire while we tempted him with savory bits and listened to his breathing. Worrying if he were in pain. Knowing if he didn't pass on his own in the next few hours, we'd be forced to cuddle him up, drive him the few miles to the vet, and help him to die.

But Touser—being the opinionated creature he was—wasn't having that.

He passed away gentle, on his own. A few hours after his girl and boys had told him goodnight...*goodbye*...and finally gone to bed.

The next day, we buried him in the yard where he'd loved to roam. Where he'd chased birds and squirrels, barking at leaves, the wind, the dogs down the way. We placed an overturned urn atop his grave, bordering it with a ring of rocks. We planted lobelia in the urn when spring finally came; watching it bloom, spreading out thick in blue, purple, and white clusters of tiny flowers. Remembering...

****

Today our Annie Rose, no longer busy with baby dolls and Barbies, still watches over Touser's grave. His best girl straightens the rock ring, brushes a light palm over the blossoms. And we talk about how happy Touser was when he was here with us—and how happy he is now. Up in Dog Heaven, where all dogs go. Even, or perhaps most especially, once-ornery, suddenly born-again, filled-with-kindness poodles.

And this is the story I tell her:

Dog Heaven?

Well—it's filled with rotten fish, and piles of bunny and turkey poop to roll in and nibble upon. And as far as the eye can see, overfull garbage cans line the streets, each ready to tip over, scatter the steaming contents, and be investigated to a canine heart's desire.

There are interesting sniffs to sniffle; soft, easy-to-dig dirt to dig; noises forever undetected by the human ear to be heard by one dog—and at once, furiously barked at by all. Abandoned shoes and pilfered sandals, baseball mitts, and lost garden hoses galore to taste and bury and dig up and run with and tug-o-war over.

The words "No," "Bad Dog," and "Leash" have never even been whispered.

A dog can howl all heavenly night, scratch up the golden doors, pee on simply anything—and no one ever even frowns.

And best of all, every evening, A Dog gets to curl up at his person's feet—or perhaps, his person's grandma's feet, if A Dog is still waiting for his person— or snuggle up against their side to watch the Heaven Sunset.

What? Well, of course there's a Heaven Sunset—and it is amazing!

There are shelled peanuts to share, and popcorn to munch. Yes—with extra butter.

And A Dog can sleep on his back with all four legs splayed in different directions with his head to one side; occasional little sleep barks and back left leg twitches the only thing disturbing his dreams.

Unless, of course, the coyotes come.

Then, A Dog jumps to his feet and Defends His Homestead despite having discovered early on the coyote pack is actually the wind singing through the trees.

Because A Dog enjoys barking a bit more than wind listening.

And when A Dog's person does eventually show up, though, it really didn't seem so long after all...

Isn't that funny?

A Dog is so happy to see her, he leaps—all four paws up, practically flying, wet-nosed, eyes gleaming.

Yipping and yelping with all the furious puppy energy

125

which is and forever was A Dog's spirit; flowing through, blending with his person's...and they talk to one another with their eyes and their smiles, just as they always have.

And the Dog's Person?

Why, look at her, just there...slipping a hand into a pocket and pulling out a dog biscuit or two. The same sort A Dog used to like best. Then, settling down side-by-side on thick grass from which the color green was taken—(Ah, but that was but a whisper of this beauty...merely a whisper.)

To watch the birds dip and soar and listen to the tree song and each other breathing steady. Yes: hearts beating, still.

To wait for the sunset; and the slow, meandering walk home.

About the Author—L.D.B. Taylor

L.D.B. Taylor (aka Lisa Taylor) is the author of several books. A lifelong reader and writer, Lisa appreciates wit, sarcasm, chocolate, hot tea, cool mountain evenings, travel, and books by the score. Website: http://www.neebeep.com/itsownsweetwillneebee pc/

MEMORIES FROM MAPLE STREET, U.S.A.—
LEAVING CHILDHOOD BEHIND

Growing up is a miraculous time. The journey from the freedom of childhood to the workaday life of becoming an adult is filled with both poignancy and wonder. Fond memories of pedaling bikes through honeysuckle-scented streets with a pack of neighborhood friends and playing "kick the can" and stickball on warm summer evenings alight with fireflies are accompanied by the inevitable loss of people and places dear to the heart—and a seminal moment when we know we're leaving childhood behind.

These are the stories of a turning point—when the world shifted, and nothing would ever be the same. In this first collection of the MEMORIES FROM MAPLE STREET, U.S.A., series, Sundown Press brings you real-life stories, from the touching to the humorous, the inspirational to the adventurous, and a wonderful group of childhood memories you'll never forget.

MEMORIES FROM MAPLE STREET, U.S.A.—THE BEST CHRISTMAS EVER

What is Christmas all about? Wonderful memories! This collection of stories celebrates the very best and most poignant memories of the past, and is sure to have you laughing and crying right along with the authors who shared their stories in MEMORIES FROM MAPLE STREET, U.S.A.—THE BEST CHRISTMAS EVER!

Sundown Press brings you a wonderful collection of heartfelt stories that you will not want to pass up—and it also makes a great gift for all ages—if you still believe in Santa!